Robert Atkins

AN UNFINISHED AUTOBIOGRAPHY

Rehearsing, 1959.

Robert Atkins

AN UNFINISHED AUTOBIOGRAPHY

Edited by
GEORGE ROWELL

With contributions from
J C TREWIN
A C SPRAGUE

The Society for Theatre Research

First published in 1994
by The Society for Theatre Research
c/o The Theatre Museum, 1E Tavistock Street
Covent Garden, London WC2E 7PA

Origination and Manufacture at The Alden Press Limited,
Northampton and Oxford, England

Contents

List of Illustrations

An Explanation

Robert Atkins constituted a rare, if not unique, link between the Edwardian theatre, with its actor-management of Tree, Forbes-Robertson, Martin Harvey and many more, and the counter-movement towards 'authentic' Shakespeare, a gospel preached by William Poel, taken up by Granville-Barker, and developed in the imaginative approach of John Gielgud and others.

The sweep of Atkins's experience in the field of Shakespeare therefore gives weight to his account of a career which stretched from 1906 to 1963, and included five seminal years as Director of Productions at the Old Vic, the foundation and sustaining of the Open Air Theatre, Regent's Park, a brief but pioneering season of Shakespeare in the round at the Blackfriars Ring and a spell as Director at the Shakespeare Memorial Theatre, Stratford-on-Avon.

Unhappily that account was begun too late and never completed. It would seem that Atkins started writing his autobiography in 1952 when he was 66, put it aside, twice resumed his work, proposed collaboration with his friend J. C. Trewin, but became increasingly uncertain of his ability to complete the task. What survives covers his training as one of the earliest students at the Academy (not yet Royal) of Dramatic Art, his apprenticeship with Tree, Harvey and Forbes-Robertson, together with a brief spell leading one of Frank Benson's touring companies, and his historic term of office at the Old Vic. Most regrettably he never wrote about his years at Regent's Park or at Stratford. The only portion covering the years after 1925 which he does seem to have completed is an account of his visit (in 1956, his stage jubilee) to the Baalbek Festival in Lebanon, and his production of the Masque of Proteus and the Adamantine Rock at Gray's Inn before Her Majesty Queen Elizabeth II, a fitting climax to fifty years of service to the theatre.

A further matter for regret is the confusion which attempting his autobiography late in life brought to the work he did complete. This is especially apparent in the chapters dealing with his touring years under Forbes-Robertson and with the Old Vic years. Correspondence with J. C. Trewin reveals that the Old Vic chapter had been 'lost' during redecoration at his home and would have to be reconstructed. That reconstruction is unhappily neither chronological nor entirely coherent, but it has been printed as it was written, rather than reshape the work of a man whose rugged individualism characterised his life as well as his career.

A substantial portion of the earliest chapter concerns his narrow (though never harsh or deprived) upbringing in the home of an uncle governed by strict Baptist principles, and since this has only negative theatrical significance it has been summarised. On the other hand his brief account of war service in Egypt and Palestine has been included, as it illustrates a theatre of war not as widely documented as that on the Western front.

As some compensation for the gaps in Atkins's own narrative, the reader is offered an extract from J. C. Trewin's account of his stewardship at Regent's Park, contributed to *Fifty Years of the Open Air Theatre, Regent's Park* (1982) and as an overall assessment of his work for Shakespeare, including his Stratford years, A. C. Sprague's essay 'Robert Atkins as a Shakespearian Director', originally published in the *Deutsche Shakespeare-Gesellschaft West Jahrbuch* in 1973. The kindness of, respectively, Wendy Trewin and the Association in allowing these reprints is gratefully acknowledged.

In his contribution to the Regent's Park record David William, one of Atkins's successors at the Open Air Theatre, writes:

> Robert's career began in the sumptuous sunset of the actor-managers Tree and Forbes-Robertson: it ended in the severer dawn of Beckett and Brecht. His acting values, therefore, were formed at Her Majesty's although he later came devotedly under the influence of William Poel. Poel's staunch Elizabethanism sounded the first notes of the trumpet that was to bring down the walls of Victorian, Imperial Shakespeare— the Shakespeare of lengthy intervals, operatic scenery, rhetorical acting and truncated texts. Robert never quite threw off a nostalgia for that kind of theatre; the puritan in him, however, the evangelist grasped the batons of Poel and Granville-Barker and carried on beyond them.

It is this conflict of principle and loyalty in the man, as much as the achievements of the actor and manager, that gives Atkins's record, however incomplete, a special appeal.

The Society for Theatre Research wishes to place on record its indebtedness to Mr. Robert Charles Atkins and Mrs. Sally Sparham for making their grandfather's account of his life available for publication.

GEORGE ROWELL

CHAPTER ONE

Early Days

Robert Atkins was born of Welsh stock on 10 August 1886 at Dulwich, South London, and shortly after his birth his family moved to Islington. His father, who had 'a promising career in the legal profession', died at the age of thirty-three, and his mother's improvident temperament consigned him when about five to the care of a kindly aunt and authoritarian uncle in Luton, Bedfordshire, where his child-hood was spent.* Their home served also as business premises (the uncle was a 'tallyman' or travelling draper and outfitter) and was conducted on strict Baptist principles. The young Atkins was never allowed any contact with the theatre, and he was only aware of its existence through reproductions of popular favourites in the pages of Home Chat *and later of the* Strand Magazine.

He derived his first acquaintance with Shakespeare from the Rev. Sass, his school instructor in religious knowledge, a clergyman who recited passages from the plays to him out of school hours and behind his uncle's back:

> We occupied a bench in a remote corner of the [recreation] ground, and after a laughing reference to himself as the 'lean and hungry', he began, quietly, explanatorily, praising the character of Brutus, but creating excitement when speaking the lines of Cassius, and at the moment of offering Brutus his dagger and naked breast, he was really carried away, and I was transported to the extent of finding myself sitting on the gravelled path, gazing rapturously, as he swayed to and fro. He sud-denly stopped, glanced over my shoulder and began fumbling the pages. The rising voice had attracted the attention of other occupants of the playing ground, and among them I noticed boys from my school, kick-ing a football around. Feeling very self-conscious, but assuming a manly stride, I walked to the gates with my mentor, who with a parting 'we must be more careful next time', strode away.

Atkins's only other exposure to the drama was from copies of Dicks' Standard Plays surreptitiously lent him by a colleague at the straw-hat manufacturers where he worked for five years after leaving school at the age of thirteen. He particularly relished Belphegor the Mountebank, *one scene from which he would enact to any available audience:*

---

* At 19 Russell Street and later at 'Gatewood', 53 Cardiff Road.

I

Punch amused its readers, at the expense of the new National Academy of Dramatic Art, with a suggested Entrance Examination Paper. Some of Mr. Punch's questions were:

Part A—For Male Candidates only.

1. How many times, and where, have you appeared in the title role of Shakespeare's *Hamlet, Prince of Denmark*? Write down as much as you can remember of the notices, if any, which you have received from the London, Suburban or Provincial Press on such occasions. State in what respects you consider your reading of the part superior to that of:
   (1) Sir Henry Irving, (2) Mr. Beerbohm Tree, (3) Mr. Forbes-Robertson, (4) Mr. Wilson Barrett.

2. What is your favourite brand of champagne? Can you, when on the stage, affect exhilaration after quaffing a bumper of effervescing ginger ale?

3. Do you prefer to provoke your audience to tears or laughter? If the former, give some idea of the facial contortions by which you would indicate (1) suspense, (2) concern, (3) agony, (4) horror, (5) despair. How do you employ your hands in each case? Have you ever performed a comic part without finding it necessary to redden your nose?

A question to lady candidates was:

Do you possess a motor car? If you were entrusted with an ingenue part at a pupils' matinee, should you insist on all your frocks being made by your own dressmaker?

Unbeknown to anyone, I applied to Mr. Tree for particulars, and the reply, to my disappointment signed by a secretary, requesting twelve guineas, closed that door of entrance to the profession. Could I save the required fee, and if all other ways of getting a start failed, apply again? Some of the six pounds was left—yes, there was a gleam of hope.

The experience of seeing E. S. Willard in *The Middleman* by Henry Arthur Jones, at the Kennington Theatre, determined me at all costs to make the theatre my future. What we would say to him today, I do not know, but his performance lives in my memory. It is possible that the adulation of his audience affected me. One must not forget that the real actor loves bowing. But his performance killed all my doubts. I wanted to act like Willard, and receive the plaudits.

Life in London did not present the comforts of the Luton existence. My bedroom was a boxroom, home life was not too orderly. My midday meal was always a meat pie, bread and butter and a cup of tea, partaken in a crowded City café, furnished with marble(?) topped tables. Every morning

CHAPTER ONE

Early Days

Robert Atkins was born of Welsh stock on 10 August 1886 at Dulwich, South London, and shortly after his birth his family moved to Islington. His father, who had 'a promising career in the legal profession', died at the age of thirty-three, and his mother's improvident temperament consigned him when about five to the care of a kindly aunt and authoritarian uncle in Luton, Bedfordshire, where his childhood was spent.* Their home served also as business premises (the uncle was a 'tallyman' or travelling draper and outfitter) and was conducted on strict Baptist principles. The young Atkins was never allowed any contact with the theatre, and he was only aware of its existence through reproductions of popular favourites in the pages of Home Chat *and later of the* Strand Magazine.

He derived his first acquaintance with Shakespeare from the Rev. Sass, his school instructor in religious knowledge, a clergyman who recited passages from the plays to him out of school hours and behind his uncle's back:

> We occupied a bench in a remote corner of the [recreation] ground, and after a laughing reference to himself as the 'lean and hungry', he began, quietly, explanatorily, praising the character of Brutus, but creating excitement when speaking the lines of Cassius, and at the moment of offering Brutus his dagger and naked breast, he was really carried away, and I was transported to the extent of finding myself sitting on the gravelled path, gazing rapturously, as he swayed to and fro. He suddenly stopped, glanced over my shoulder and began fumbling the pages. The rising voice had attracted the attention of other occupants of the playing ground, and among them I noticed boys from my school, kicking a football around. Feeling very self-conscious, but assuming a manly stride, I walked to the gates with my mentor, who with a parting 'we must be more careful next time', strode away.

Atkins's only other exposure to the drama was from copies of Dicks' Standard Plays surreptitiously lent him by a colleague at the straw-hat manufacturers where he worked for five years after leaving school at the age of thirteen. He particularly relished Belphegor the Mountebank, *one scene from which he would enact to any available audience:*

* At 19 Russell Street and later at 'Gatewood', 53 Cardiff Road.

I

BELPHEGOR: What's the matter, Henri?

HENRI: Sister's no longer in her little bed, and mama's not there.

BELPHEGOR: Nonsense! Nonsense! What childishness. (*Quick exit and return with a piece of paper*) Am I asleep? Or is my brain turning? (*Reading*) 'Guillaume, adieu! Forgive me, forgive me.' Gone! She's gone, Henri; you have no longer a Mother; you have no longer a sister! Madeline has left us all alone, all alone, my child, all alone. Oh, Henri, I have no one now but you in the world, Henri! I'm choking—suffocating—speak to me, Henri—let me hear your voice—you don't know how (*faltering*) how I loved her.

HENRI: (*unloosing his neck-handkerchief*) Father! Father! Open your eyes! Let me hear your voice—one word, only one. Oh, Mother, Mother, you've killed him! I hate and detest you!

BELPHEGOR: (*recovering himself, stops him*) No, child, no; not a word more; join your hands to mine, and let us pray for her; pray—pray! (*Both kneel in an attitude of prayer. BELPHEGOR, with an effort, falls senseless.*)

Eventually his uncle allowed him an occasional visit to London to receive instruction from Ian Forbes, actor-brother of Johnston Forbes-Robertson:

On the day appointed, following written instructions, I found my way, via Saint Pancras, where, upon alighting, I wanted to take the next train back, to the rooms above a corner picture shop near the British Museum. An elderly lady answered my trembling knock, and showed me into the sitting room, where I sat for some minutes before Mr. Robertson entered, a tall, thin man, wearing black and white check trousers, and black coat and waistcoat. A wicked pity came through his smile, and bidding me be seated, he placed himself before the fireplace and assailed me with a long tirade against the theatre, the final censure being that his own brother, a wonderful actor, after years of struggle, was a poor man. Tea intervened, and during my nervous gulpings he questioned me kindly about my education. The replies did not help. Did I know any Shakespeare? The Dream of Clarence came to my aid, and when I had finished, he cocked an eye of interest, and plucking a book from the shelves, he recited Austin Dobson's poem, 'The Carver and the Caliph'. The book was thrust into my hands, with instructions to return, same day, same time, with the poem memorised. He would then, upon hearing me recite it, deliver judgment.

2

... The outcome was an offer to give me twelve weekly lessons and then advise. Eventual association with Ian Forbes-Robertson exposed his dislike of the theatre as a profession, and his great brother, Sir Johnston, told me himself that he disliked acting. During this period of instruction I did not once put my foot inside a London theatre; the time of the return train was marked.

... Robertson helped me with the pieces with varying enthusiasm, but I waited in vain for 'Yes, my boy, go on the stage'. Was he conspiring with the people at home? There the glories of an amateur status were the hintings of my Aunt. Robertson's suggestion that when the time came, I might carry a banner in the opening production at the new Scala Theatre met with indecision on my part. I was frightened, I didn't want to leave the dove-cote ... A good thing, perhaps, for *The Conqueror*, the opening play, proved a failure, and I might have been back in Luton with many an 'I told you so' ringing in my ears.

Atkins's restlessness persisted and in the autumn of 1904, when he was eighteen, he persuaded his uncle to agree to his moving to London, where he was to lodge with other relatives, and where he would be able to pursue his passion for the theatre unchecked.

Letters passed between my Aunt and her sister Nelly, who, having married a not too well-to-do retired sea-captain, offered me a roof for the time being.

And so the day came when, with an inherited feeling for the stage, and little to show for my school education, with a certain knowledge of, and a deep love for music, a worthwhile baritone singing voice, a smattering of literature, for which may God bless Hemmings,* and with six pounds in my pocket, the proceeds of the sale of my bicycle, I turned my back on Luton. I had no plans, and the one theatrical person I knew, Mr. Robertson, was, I discovered by letter, away on tour. And so, with 'Good Luck's' from the warehouse, but no blessings from the family—they fondly hoped to prepare a calf—the train puffed me into the future. That night I cried myself to sleep, wishing to God that I was back in my own bed.

LONDON

In my new home, in Stockwell, S.W., the theatre was talked about with enthusiasm by two members of the household, Charles and Fanny Jolly, step-son and step-daughter of my Aunt Nelly. In the kindness of their hearts they had given my mother a much-needed roof, so through my precipitate action in leaving Luton, mother and son were at last together. My dear

---

*His supervisor at work, who encouraged his literary interests.

mother had never overtaken life since her husband died, and never did. Three passions possessed her—Dickens, Irving and Ellen Terry—and Tennyson was no stranger. Lovely of face and with a beautiful figure that she took to the grave, her bitterness was, she should have been an actress. Her consolation was often London porter.

My new uncle, John, retired captain Jolly of the Nelson Line, did not belie his name—a stocky, broad-shouldered man, with a face that would have done duty on the title page of *Punch*. He expressed sympathy with my aspirations, but advised, 'Caution, take time, get a business job and look around the theatre". He really hoped that I would go back to Luton.

His son and daughter were theatre mad. Charles, a law clerk, hoped to be a singer and was taking lessons with the then well-known Randegger. Fanny, a teacher under the London School Board, was an enthusiastic member of the Birkbeck amateur society and was fondly hoping to be picked up by a management. In the early days of my new life, they were inclined to talk down to their country cousin. The 'Mouse' attained his ambition, they remained on the auditorium side of the curtain. But they were good souls and treated me to many a pit and gallery.

Following Uncle John's advice I answered many advertisements, finding myself one morning in the waiting room of Debenham and Co., St. Paul's Churchyard. A kindly gentleman interviewed me, but my inability to work out quickly a fractional sum saw the doors kindly close behind me.

Letters went to managers, some were answered, some were not, many of the 'not' ones, I am sure, because of my finishing lines—'my deep desire to serve the art I love so well'. In answer to an advertisement in a now defunct theatrical paper *The Era*, I waited upon a gentleman (an agent) occupying a top floor office in Garrick Street. He was a small man, with a pallid face and well oiled black hair. With a gesture, a good one, he bade me be seated, and proceeded, while questioning me, to pace the floor, breaking the pacing to gaze heavenwards through the window as though seeking inspiration. It came: he had the very idea, I was cut out to put over a 'Song Scene'. Realising that I had not the slightest idea of what the title meant, he explained dramatically: The curtain is down, the orchestra is playing soft and mysterious music, the curtain rises and I am discovered, in a shack, sitting at a table with head bowed on arm. I lift my head, I rise, I go towards the shuttered window and fling the shutters open. The glittering moonlight falls upon me, and the audience realise by the backcloth that I am in farthest Canada, far away from home. Tears come into my eyes, I turn towards the audience, meanwhile the orchestra has begun the opening bars of the song (yet to be composed) that I am to burst into—a song of home.

4

The gentleman was sure he could fix me an opening date at Greenwich, and in the meantime, would fix a seat for me at the Canterbury Music Hall, where I could see a famous performer of Song Scenes in action. Also in the meantime would I leave a few shillings for postage. He was so agile in my interest that within a week I received, on a postcard, a request for more shillings. I did not oblige.

My descent upon London was made at a time inopportune for job-hunting in the theatre. As was the custom then, many of the theatres closed during the summer weeks and the managements were busy preparing the autumn productions. These preparations caused me to perform a ritual known only to myself. I would walk the Strand, pausing in front of the Vaudeville and Adelphi theatres, and imagine what was going on inside. Then passing into Maiden Lane, I would gaze at the stage door of the Adelphi, where William Terriss was stabbed to death. The pilgrimage finished at the shrine of His Majesty's theatre. Always, in my imagination, my theatrical debut was to be here. The manager had been favoured with a letter, and I had received the usual regrets. One morning I summoned up enough courage to enter the stage door, and came face to face with a man in uniform who wished to know my business. His tone was kindly, he was sure that there were no vacancies for the *Tempest* that was in the course of preparation. Would I like to peep at the stage? I did peep, and saw the carpenters building a large ship. I was put at ease and advised that Mr. Tree was opening a school for acting. Alas, I had no money. I was ushered from the stage door, with 'good luck's' and a suggestion to try touring. The commissionaire recalled the conversation to me when I attended my first professional rehearsal.

The autumn of 1904 found me in the London office of a Manchester firm dealing with art needlework, at an emolument of nineteen shillings a week. This enabled me to contribute something towards my keep, but the hours, eight-thirty to five-thirty, and one o'clock on Saturdays, left me no time for tackling the theatre. Anyway, I was running round in circles, for writing letters and haunting stage doors was the only conceivable approach. Touring advertisements in *The Era* told me that it was necessary to 'dress well, on and off', a condition that ruled me out. Twice, my letters caused touring managers to write me to wait upon them, with the result, 'Come again when you have had experience.' The same story, then as now.

My newly found 'cousin', Charles Jolly, through his association with Randegger, hobnobbed with professionals of sorts and reported upon the sarcastic professional attitude towards Mr. Tree's newly founded 'School of Acting'.

5

Punch amused its readers, at the expense of the new National Academy of Dramatic Art, with a suggested Entrance Examination Paper. Some of Mr. Punch's questions were:

Part A—For Male Candidates only.

1. How many times, and where, have you appeared in the title role of Shakespeare's *Hamlet, Prince of Denmark?* Write down as much as you can remember of the notices, if any, which you have received from the London, Suburban or Provincial Press on such occasions. State in what respects you consider your reading of the part superior to that of:
   (1) Sir Henry Irving, (2) Mr. Beerbohm Tree, (3) Mr. Forbes-Robertson, (4) Mr. Wilson Barrett.

2. What is your favourite brand of champagne? Can you, when on the stage, affect exhilaration after quaffing a bumper of effervescing ginger ale?

3. Do you prefer to provoke your audience to tears or laughter? If the former, give some idea of the facial contortions by which you would indicate (1) suspense, (2) concern, (3) agony, (4) horror, (5) despair. How do you employ your hands in each case? Have you ever performed a comic part without finding it necessary to redden your nose?

A question to lady candidates was:

Do you possess a motor car? If you were entrusted with an ingenue part at a pupils' matinee, should you insist on all your frocks being made by your own dressmaker?

Unbeknown to anyone, I applied to Mr. Tree for particulars, and the reply, to my disappointment signed by a secretary, requesting twelve guineas, closed that door of entrance to the profession. Could I save the required fee, and if all other ways of getting a start failed, apply again? Some of the six pounds was left—yes, there was a gleam of hope.

The experience of seeing E. S. Willard in *The Middleman* by Henry Arthur Jones, at the Kennington Theatre, determined me at all costs to make the theatre my future. What we would say to him today, I do not know, but his performance lives in my memory. It is possible that the adulation of his audience affected me. One must not forget that the real actor loves bowing. But his performance killed all my doubts. I wanted to act like Willard, and receive the plaudits.

Life in London did not present the comforts of the Luton existence. My bedroom was a boxroom, home life was not too orderly. My midday meal was always a meat pie, bread and butter and a cup of tea, partaken in a crowded City café, furnished with marble(?) topped tables. Every morning at 7.45 I would wait in a crowd (orderly queuing was not observed then), by the White Horse, Stockwell, and mount the upper deck of the horse-drawn omnibus. Oh! joy, if lucky enough to gain that exclusive seat next to the driver. What characters the drivers were, with their glazed bowler hats, the ribbon on the whips, the buttonhole, and their cockney terms of endearment and admonition to their horses. On alighting, I would join the pavement throngs swarming into the City and, entering the narrow thoroughfare named Rose Street, would pass into the realms of Art Needlework.

I never regretted the few months in Rose Street. Invoicing was part of the job, and remembering my past misdemeanors in the world of figures, I took over with trepidation, but, miracle of miracles, I found myself able to put two and two together with more fluency and exactitude than of old. The managing man was unimaginative, and mad on the game of Lacrosse. His censure blasted one with its North Country forthrightness.

The stool next to mine was occupied by a tall, pale-faced, herring-gutted youth, who entertained the people of his suburb by singing popular songs of the period. When the boss was out he would practise them, much to the satisfaction of the girl clerk, who adored him. It was a terrible voice, but during the 1930s, when I was visiting a show at the Devonshire Park, Eastbourne, a very stout fellow introduced himself as the boy who sat with me in the office in Rose Street. He was a member of the Concert Party.

As the junior member of the office I was often sent on errands, to my joy, for I could slip into Newgate Street and gaze upon the building in which Henry Irving had been employed as a clerk, walk around St. Paul's Churchyard and see the names, Smith and Lister, Cook, Son and Co., and Hitchcock Williams, firms to whom I had despatched many boxes of hats. I dodged the buses and hansom cabs on Cheapside and Ludgate Hill, and when I thought I could explain away a longish absence, would open a few books in Paternoster Row. Foregoing the meat pie, I visited the Guildhall Picture Gallery and found the Onslow Ford statue of Irving as Hamlet, and the interior of St. Paul's Cathedral was explored under pieless conditions. I don't remember seeing people eating sandwiches under the Dome as they do today.

While, like the varlets in Shakespeare's play, *The Tempest*, I was 'bending towards my project' (forgive the misquotation), Mr. Joseph Chamberlain was voicing his Protection policy, and the Russo–Japanese War was raging in the Far East. England had been roused by the Russian outrage on British trawling boats, and Mr. Balfour had made a very strong speech on the situation. Hans Richter, Madame Calvé and Signor Caruso had delighted audiences at Covent Garden, and England had recovered the Ashes.

Of more interest to me was the minority attack on Mr. Tree, for producing *The Tempest* as a pantomime. The Elizabethans of 1904 were stirring. I had not read, or seen a performance of *The Tempest* and was ignorant of the existence of such bodies as 'The London Shakespeare League' and 'The Elizabethan Stage Society'. But cousin Fanny, whose occupation gave her knowledge of the work of the Rev. Stewart Headlam, who was interested in both of the societies, reported a statement made by him upon 'The Staging of Shakespeare':

> To succeed, Shakespeare must be done in the Elizabethan manner, without scenery and, where possible, with the exits and entrances into the auditorium from the stage. We have to deliver Shakespeare from his two greatest enemies—the scene-painter and scene-builder on the one hand, and the student or lecturer on the other, who thinks that Shakespeare can be understood in the armchair. By leaving Shakespeare to be dealt with in the Elizabethan way you are able to get the whole play acted in a reasonable time, and to get it acted with the actors properly balanced; the play is then indeed the thing.

The controversy is hot on the wing in 1952, and I happen to be one of the modern pioneers for restoring the Shakespeare plays to the style of theatre for which they were written.

Eventually I saw Mr. Tree's production of *The Tempest* from the 'Good Old Pit' of His Majesty's Theatre, and my youthful eyes were entranced by the stage settings, and the comic animals delighted me. In no way was I competent to judge the speaking of the play, nor, for that matter, the rightness or wrongness of the production, but with William Haviland, Lyn Harding, Fisher White and Louis Calvert in the cast, gentlemen with whom I was destined to be associated, the speaking must have been on a high level. A copy of Mr. Tree's answer to his critics, dated 1904, is in my possession. Today, I do not altogether agree with all the arguments favouring his methods.

After Henry Irving, Mr. Tree did not appeal to my mother, but the visit to the theatre reminded her of an old friend who had played small parts with Tree at the Haymarket. I begged her to track him down. Mother was not at all enthusiastic about the future I was planning, but with the hope of an introduction to Mr. Tree, we eventually took tea with Mr. Orme. The request was turned down: he would not help me in any way, the theatre was a lousy profession. Mr. Orme's son became a successful actor, under the name of Philip Tonge.

The new family circle was no more encouraging to my pursuit of the theatre than were the 'Gateside' folk. Both parties hoped that I would tire, and that Luton would have the honour of killing the fatted calf. But the London scene was breeding a confidence in myself. A direct entrance into the profession seemed as far away as ever, so the dim hope of amassing sufficient funds to apply for entrance to Tree's school became a flickering beacon light. To this end I was saving four or five shillings a week. Seven shillings of my nineteen went to board and lodging, and the midday snack and fares depleted the remainder, so to help matters I sometimes walked from the City to Stockwell, little thinking of the pennies required for shoe repairs.

In my discovery of London, I think I knew every stage door in the theatre regions, through applying to the 'door keepers' for news of vacancies—a stupid procedure, but I did not know. Some were kind, some were not. One advised me to see Mr. Blackmore, the agent on Garrick Street. A bilious attack was the excuse for my absence from Rose Street on the morning of my approach to Mr. Blackmore. A number of people were passing up and down the stairway that led up to the offices, and in the doorway of one stood a gentleman, rubbing his hands with glee and voicing, 'Nothing today, nothing today, nothing'. One voice in the endless belt of applicants cried, 'Gawd, it's been like this for weeks'. Many living members of the profession will remember a partner, Mr. Nicholls, and his 'Nothing today'.

I was no longer dependent upon the illustrated papers for an acquaintance with the wonders of London. I found the City churches, and a Sunday morning visit to Rotten Row to watch the mounted gentry exercising, with a hope that I might see a well-known actor on horseback, stimulated the feeling that one day I would be pictured in the papers as the well-known actor riding in the Row. The Church Parade in Kensington Gardens struck me as rather stupid.

Cousin Charles, a good Londoner, showed me where Astley's Amphitheatre stood, and with him I sampled performances at the South London and Canterbury Music Halls. One day we went down Hoxton way. The 'Old Brit' was no more, but Mr. Pollock was 'all alive O' with his 'Penny plain and twopenny coloured'. Alas, the 'Coloured Sheets' and 'Cut Grottoes', from the 'Theatrical Juvenile Pollock Print Warehouse' belong to the past, and the modern juvenile is poorer by the loss of a fascinating toy. But I bear Hoxton a grudge, for through a family quarrel, my mother's step-sister left a considerable sum of money to the Hoxton Branch of the Salvation Army.

With Charles I heard my first Promenade Concert, at the Queen's Hall, under the then Mr. Henry Wood. This first experience of listening to and seeing an orchestra revived my musical ambition. Oh, to be a Henry Wood.

There was no piano at the Stockwell home and apart from warbling a few musical scales I was musically stranded. Charles practised at the home of the girl he was courting, and I disgraced myself on the one and only occasion of a visit to her home to enjoy a musical evening. Her father, a manufacturer of carriage lamps, had, in his youth, attempted the stage, and had acted at Sadlers Wells with E. H. Brooke, son of the great Brooke, and during the evening in question, obliged with a dramatic piece. He spoke as follows:

I le-hooked to-hard the de-hoor,
And what did I se-hee—a ge-host.

I laughed, and was never invited again.

Saturday night was queuing night for a theatre pit or gallery. There were no stools, and if the play were popular, the wait was a lengthy business. The 'Gallery First Nighters Club' was a few years old, and strictly adhered to the Club ruling, that 'Genuine gallery playgoers alone are eligible for membership'. I doubt if the 1952 President of the Club, the delightful and enthusiastic Leslie Bloom, has ever watched a play from the gallery. I don't blame him, for I have always considered the average theatre gallery to be a pernicious viewing place. Certainly, in the 'good old days', the actor was trained to throw the voice to the shilling patrons in the 'Gods'. The two and sixpenny 'Pitites', seated on floor level behind the stalls, had a grand view of both stage and the stalls, and latecomers of the classy set were under no misapprehension as to what the 'Pitites' thought of them.

The queuers, drawn from the middle classes, were a matey lot, and were primed in the gossip of the theatre. The gossip did not extend to the brand of soap used by a particular actress. Hysterical? Well, there was a constancy exhibited by the females who belonged to the 'Keen on Waller Brigade'. I suppose Lewis Waller was the first actor to receive a fan mail. I first saw Waller as Henry V, at the Imperial Theatre. The voices of Henry Ainley, in *Merely Mary Ann*, and of Basil Gill, in *The Tempest*, had thrilled me, but the voice of Waller was a revelation. This quality, plus his virility and chivalrous bearing, captivated me, and, incompetent as I was to judge, his performance to me was it.

The memory of *San Toy* was not effaced by *The Catch of the Season*, but the 'Gibson Girl' in the play, as presented by Miss Camille Clifford, was an intriguing figure.

Prior to my leaving the town, the theatre hoardings at Luton announced the visit of 'The Rising Young Tragedian', Cyril D'Este. The background colour of the bills was a violent yellow, the type in black. *Hamlet, Macbeth* and *Romeo and Juliet* were among the plays to be presented, but D'Este was the dominating piece of the printing. In my mind's eye, the future was to change that name—no, not Alec, the name I was known by, but my second name, Robert—and the bills would read 'The Rising Young Tragedian, Robert Atkins'.

The Tragic Muse accompanied me to London, and my early associates of the theatre regarded me as a very serious young man. My mother said I was pompous. Perhaps I was, in the home. I disliked the unmethodical way the household was run. Strange to say, I was missing the clockwork method of 'Gateside'.

The family background was filtering through. During quarrels, and they were many, Aunt Nelly would accuse my mother of always lacking method and therefore having ruined her life. Aunt Miriam's deceased husband would have been a brilliant doctor, but for drink and socialism. He had been arrested in Trafalgar Square for attempting to interest a crowd in Marxism. Of my father I learned little. To Aunt Nelly he was a very lovely man. My dear mother was reluctant to speak of him, but the serious side of his nature seemed to have oppressed her. Aunties Miriam and Mary were eking out a living serving in dairy shops, and the news from my brother, now farming in Africa, told of failure. I *was* serious, but not methodical, and have never been blessed with that quality.

My limited knowledge of the plays of Shakespeare confined the dramatist to the serious and tragic vein, and a shock was administered when witnessing the Adelphi production of *The Taming of the Shrew*, with Oscar Asche and Lily Brayton in the leading roles. Here was a Shakespeare I did not know. Three times I visited the gallery to revel in the fun of that delightful presentation. Has a better performance of this play been given since? I doubt it.

The splendour of the production of *Much Ado about Nothing* at His Majesty's did not escape me, but the play did. This worried me, and talking it over with my mother I was given a picture of the Henry Irving/Ellen Terry performance. I then, for the first time, read the play, and with a glimmer of understanding, put a question to my mother. Why did Mr. Tree, as Benedick, climb into the branch of a tree in order to overhear the conversation of the conspirators, instead of entering an arbour as directed by the dramatist, and, incidentally, why did he shake down oranges on the heads of the men below him in order to get laughter? 'Oh,' came the answer, 'Mr. Tree is a buffoon.'

This first exercise in pitting the text against performance made me wonder why the actor playing the Prince, Don Pedro, presented him as a rather common person. But buffoon or no buffoon, Mr. Tree's theatre via Gower

Street was still my goal, and to that end the spring of 1905 found me keeping my end up at Rose Street and scraping the shillings together. Advice from the Stockwell home and letters from my aunt at Luton urged me to foreswear the theatre; well, 'witness the reluctance of managers and agents to recognise your histrionic abilities.'

A trumpet sounded in the gallery queue in which I was waiting to see *The Walls of Jericho* at the Garrick Theatre. 'I see in the paper,' said one woman to another, 'that the fees at Tree's School of Acting are coming down.' The discomfort of the gallery was forgotten as the overheard remark turned in my brain. If true, would the revised fee meet my slender means? The following morning I searched the Sunday *Referee* in vain. Not a word did I say to anyone. During the week I was on the carpet at Rose Street for absent-mindedness. At last, in desperation, absenting myself from the office, I knocked upon the door of number 62, Gower Street. Is there a finer body of men than the Corps of Commissionaires? Whether acting as guardian to a stage door, escorting a lady from a fur store to her carriage, or as represented by Henderson, the doorkeeper of Mr. Tree's Academy.

He listened to my story, his small crinkled face beaming with sympathy. Bidding me wait, he disappeared. I knew I had found a friend, and then his voice bade me to 'Step this way, Sir.'

Was I to see Mr. Tree? No! Behind a desk, in a rather gloomy room, stood a small gentleman with black wavy hair, black eyebrows and black beady eyes. His handshake, and gesture bidding me be seated, gave me assurance and my tale flowed easily. I received the usual warnings, the precariousness of the Profession, and a picture of the changing times, it was no longer as easy to get one's training in provincial companies, as in the old days, but as the son of an actor, he sympathised with aspirants. My look of enquiry prompted him to tell me that he was the son of Sir Squire and Lady Bancroft, who acted under the name of Marie Wilton. I wanted to sink under the floor; their history was unknown to me. Then followed the story of his mother and the 'Blood Tub' Theatre in Tottenham Street.

Coming back to my own affairs, my heart fluttered as he approached ways and means. The fee would be six guineas a term. 'Yes, I could pay that.' 'And have you sufficient money to live on?' asked Mr. Bancroft. 'Yes,' I stammered, 'my family will help me.' 'You are sure?' he continued. 'Yes,' I replied, concealing the fact that I had not given a thought to my upkeep, and was not at all sure that the family would help. Then I was on my feet, in answer to Mr. Bancroft's request for a taste of my quality. 'Ah! this is the test,' I thought, and began, 'Edinburgh After Flodden, a poem, by William

Edmondstoune Aytoun,' and was halted on the line 'Save when kings or heroes die', and I wanted to die on hearing that I would be advised of the date of the official test and full details. I was ushered from the room with compliments upon my voice and the hope that if all went well, I would enter the Academy for the April term. The Sergeant wished me good luck, and hoped that he would be seeing a lot of me soon.

The boss gave me a very queer look on my return to the office in the afternoon and remarked that my absenteeism was becoming a habit, and perhaps treatment under a doctor would help me. I saw the red light, and would have to watch my step in order to scrape a few more shillings together before the summons came for the Audition. Nine pounds was the sum total of my wealth, and I decided to be ill no more during office hours and stake all on Gower Street.

Springtime had arrived, and Saturday afternoons would find me on Clapham Common, exercising my breathing, in ways given me by Mr. Heath, and, when out of earshot of other mortals, giving vent vocally. The now determined course was my own secret; when the time came I would storm the family castle.

The awaited notification arrived, giving me three weeks' grace. That day the office did not receive my full attention. My mood alternated between hope and despair, my Luton uncle might or might not help me to scrape along. 'But surely,' I thought, 'my being able to pay the fee would weigh with him.' Before the office closed I was on the carpet; mistakes had been made, the boss was not satisfied, and I blurted out the truth, and under a sudden impulse—maybe a lifelong fault—said I would like to leave that night. The world of Art Needlework dispensed with my services with alacrity.

On the way home I paused before the building in which Henry Irving had worked as a clerk and asked for heavenly help and was encouraged to lay my plans before the Stockwell family that night. My mother said I was a fool, Uncle Jolly was sorrowful, and thought I had been a little precipitate in leaving Rose Street, Aunt Nelly twittered, thinking a good talk would help, and Charles and Fanny patted me on the shoulder, admiring my courage, but I don't think they had much hope for my future. They all thought that Luton would turn down my appeal for help, but I made the arrangements to face the music, and if lucky, would stay there and study the set piece for the Audition which was 'Othello's Address to the Senate'. The two other items were a piece chosen by myself and reading at sight.

Aunt Maggie received me with embraces that suggested that I would never leave home again, and Uncle seemed very pleased to see me. But I had not warned them of the reason for my sudden arrival and with a daring that surprised myself, unfolded the situation.

It was a blow to them; they thought I was beaten. The following day, Mr. Hyder and Roland* were called in for consultation, the upshot being that if I wished to waste my six guineas, I would be allowed seven shillings a week upon which to live. Eureka! Aunt Nelly had accepted seven shillings a week while I was at Rose Street and I was sure she would help me again. Besides, there would be three pounds odd over after I had paid the fee, and that would help towards bus fares and the midday snack.

The grassy slopes and hedgerows of the Dunstable Downs provided the necessary quietude for rehearsing the Othello speech, except on one occasion when my 'Most potenting' was stopped by the appearance of a man's head above a low hedge and the sound of a terrible voice requesting me not to disturb his sleep with my something shouting. 'What are you anyway, a bloody parson?' I ran like hell!

During Uncle's absence from the house, Auntie would listen to me, but her approbation was tinged with sorrow. On the other hand, Mrs. Walsh was all enthusiasm and helped me to decide upon Dobson's 'The Carver and the Caliph' for my chosen piece.

My wardrobe was a sorry array, but Uncle was persuaded to give me a new suit and two shirts—from the shop. He maintained a stony silence on the subject of my future. I was 'A Blot on the "Scutcheon".'

The fatal day arrived. I remember little of my emotions as I passed through the test, nor the names of those who sat in judgment. One memory is bright, the meeting, on the doorstep, with S. J. Warmington, a fellow aspirant to fame. We were both bowler-hatted, and shook hands nervously after self introductions. He was my first friend in my new world, a friendship that remained steadfast until Hitler's bombs deprived him of his life while he was doing valiant rescue work during a raid on London.

As an Officer in the Guards he served his country well in the first world war, bearing, it was reported, a charmed life. Warmy, or Sam, as he was known, was an erudite and an amusing fellow, warm-hearted and cold-blooded by turns; when fortune smiled upon him, snobbery peeped out. Generous to a fault with his own and other people's money, he turned a deaf ear, like many of us, to the advice of Polonius upon 'borrowing and lending.'

My last sight of him was in a Gloucester Road pub. He was in truculent mood. A sour and churlish tendency, engendered by a long period of professional disappointment, was sweetened by the charm and help of his newly-wed wife. Brandishing a glass of whisky and soda, he shouted to me, 'I owe you money, don't I? Yes, you think you'll get it, don't you? Yes—well

* A headmaster and his son, neighbours.

you bloody well won't, so what?' Within a week or two, he was crushed by the falling column of a Kensington portico. A very dear and irritating friend.

I passed the test, parted with my six guineas, the Stockwell home agreed to house me again, and on 5 April 1905, I became one of a group scoffed at by the old professionals, a student at Mr. Tree's Academy. Anyway, one foot was on the first rung of the theatrical ladder.

CHAPTER TWO

Mr. Tree's Academy

THE *Punch* notice of Stephen Phillips' play *Nero*, produced at His Majesty's Theatre in January 1906, contained this paragraph:

> I do not know if the ladies and gentlemen who take the small speaking parts and those who swell the crowd are pupils of the dramatic school in which Mr. Tree teaches acting in all its branches, but anyhow they are the most promising pupils, and do thorough justice to their able instructor.

I proudly regard this as my first press notice, as I was one of the four chosen to swell the crowd. Payment was at the supers' rate of 2s 6d per performance but with my 7/- a week from Luton, I was a rich man, and on Friday nights when the 'ghost walked', a term seldom used today, I would instruct the dresser to include me in the rum ration, a large glass of hot rum from the 'Cabin' in the alley opposite the stage door, price 4d.

Swelling the crowd eight times a week and attending classes in Gower Street was living life to the full, hard and tearing as it was, but the experience of 'walking on' before an audience gave one a confidence in class work that was invaluable.

This was not my first appearance. In October 1905, my second term at the Academy, Mr. Tree revived Ibsen's *An Enemy of the People* for three special matinees. A few of us were allowed to fill up the corners in the public meeting scene, out instructions were to dislike Dr. Stockmann and at certain cues to boo, bah, or rubbish. Rehearsals were few and for us limited to the one scene, so the memory of the occasion is blurred.

One memory of the first performance is vivid. The revival occurred a few days after the Liberal party had been returned to power under Campbell Bannerman and when Mr. Tree as Stockmann, addressing the meeting, spoke the lines 'The most dangerous foe to truth and freedom in our midst is the compact majority. Yes, it's the confounded compact, liberal majority— that and nothing else—there I've told you.' Hell seemed to break loose in the auditorium—cheers and countercheers, booing. The play was held up for some minutes. Tree has been termed a man of delightful contradictions. As the founder of the RADA I think the term sticks.

His answer to the question, 'Can acting be taught?' was always a categorical NO, triumphing in his own quick transit from the amateur stage to leading parts and management as a professional. To him acting was purely an affair of the imagination and he decried those who considered technique to be the end and aim of art.

Yet I well remember, it was after a *Nero* rehearsal, how he chatted to us students and begged us to take advantage of the instructions given to us by the brilliant teachers he had attracted to the Academy, actors and actresses trained under the old Stock Company system, and complained that but for his father's dislike of his wishing to become a professional actor he would have joined the Stocks instead of floundering about with amateurs and then entering the profession without a technical command of voice and body. It is recorded that in 1892 Tree was concerned with the lack of, as he termed it, the recruiting ground for the young actor.

The Stock companies were disappearing and long runs were prevailing in London. His idea was a school of fencing, dancing and elocution.

In 1904, a little against his will I believe, but under pressure from professional and other friends who were concerned with the increasing lack of training facilities for budding talent, Tree founded what is now the flourishing RADA. As Lady Tree termed it, a sturdy branch of the parent Tree.

Mr. Tree's 'School of Acting' began its life in the famous Dome of His Majesty's Theatre. By the time I joined in April 1905, the school had moved to 62 Gower Street. Today, 400 students a term are registered including many entries from abroad. In 1905 less than a hundred assembled and only one from abroad, a New Zealander, Frederick Lloyd, who became famous as a broadcaster. In 1906 the first American appeared, Cecil Yap.

The facade of the modern RADA will never in my mind replace the big brass knocker which hung upon the Victorian door behind which hung our hopes and fears. Hopes and fears—during the rehearsals for *An Enemy of the People*, hard up old actors 'swelling the crowd' would buttonhole us students and hiss warning poison into our ears. 'How dare you enter our profession through the society door, get out into the provinces and learn the hard way laddie, learn the hard way, you can't learn to act in a drawing room.'

Maiden Lane still echoed with the footsteps of the astrakhan-collared actor who poured scorn upon the idea of a school of acting. Many of Tree's associates doubted the innovation. He himself did not believe that an academy could replace the stock and touring training but did think, as they were disappearing, that under the guidance of experienced members of the profession, the fundamentals could be imparted.

And what a galaxy of artists gathered round him to help the innovation. James Fernandez, Fred Kerr, J. Fisher White, Mrs. Kate Crowe, Cavalazzi for

Mime, Bertrand for fencing and often Adeline Genée would pop in to inspect the gavotte and minuet. Some of them doubtful of the experiment, but loyal to the founder of the institution, kindly but severe to his pupils.

They had all learned the hard way and we experienced a feeling of the method. The great ones did not despise us: Hare, Alexander, Du Maurier, Sir Squire and Lady Bancroft, Barrie, Pinero would often look in to give advice and encouragement. My first memory of Mr. Tree was of him addressing the students of my first term, frock-coated, sandy hair, blue eyes, the right hand on his hip and one leg bent. He finished his welcome by saying he wished he could have Hamlet's advice to the players printed in words of gold and a copy hung in each room of the Academy.

In the year 1925 when I first worked with Sir Arthur Pinero, he told me that he was partly responsible for introducing high society into a professional cast in 1898. During my terms at the Academy society was not represented. There were a few fur coats—I remember Ruby Miller's, but she lived on Brixton Hill, and Iris Hoey was always nicely clad—in my memory we were a middle class bunch, with a tinge of the upper cut, finding our way home on the horse-drawn bus or tram. The more well to do would sometimes have a hansom cab, growlers were not popular, and of course if they plied on one's route a ride on the newly introduced motor buses was an excitement.

Oxford or Cambridge were not represented and although Arthur Bourchier, then successful at the Garrick Theatre as an actor manager, had been responsible when an undergraduate for founding the OUDS, he did not take any interest in his brother actor manager's experiment. Gossip had it that the twain did not meet. We were a very happy band of brothers and sisters at the Academy 1905–6 and there seemed to be a communal desire to do well for the Master's sake because we knew that scorn and contempt were hurled at his venture by many professionals. We often wondered what our reception would be when we stepped into the theatre world and said 'we are from Mr. Tree's Academy.'

In January 1906 when the chosen few entered the profession, swelling the crowd in *Nero*, a warm but critical welcome was given us by the cast. Mr. J. Fisher White, a member of the company, and one of our tutors, had prepared the way. Ha, what a magnificent actor he was, heart and soul behind the school experiment. Mr. Tree welcomed us with anxious eyes. The story had gone the rounds that a brother manager had said to him, 'Tree, I have a student from your school in my next play'. Tree answered, 'Oh!, You're lucky, I have two.'

Esmé Percy, the 'Britannicus' in the play who had in 1905 caused a stir by his performance of Romeo under William Poel's Elizabethan direction at the

Royalty Theatre, was keenly interested in our school experience—he had studied under Sarah Bernhardt. Lyn Harding, who had walked the streets of Cardiff as a police constable, took me under his wing when I told him that my mother was Welsh. Basil Gill, the matinee idol of Tree's company, was very friendly and C. W. Somerset, what a comedian—an avowed enemy of the school—would frighten us with his gargoyle face as he grumbled bawdy imprecations on the drawing room actors. But behind the antagonism lay a warm heart and he gave us many useful tips, the advice being well punctuated with foul words.

Drawing room actors we were, for the theatre at 62 Gower Street was the drawing room floor, two rooms knocked into one with a platform 18 inches high at one end of the stage. The performers' access to the stage was one door opening from the passage-way. A curtain surround and one traverse stood for scenery and two floodlights the lighting. There was no attempt at production from a scenic or lighting angle, just rehearsing speech and movement upon a platform. But we had to speak as though we were in a large theatre and move as upon a large stage. Most of the work was under daylight conditions. Imagination was the key word, a valuable situation in training.

The curriculum was Fencing, Dancing, Mime, body control under the Delsarte system, vocal training, and rehearsal classes. The comparatively small number of students then made individual attention by the tutors possible. Mass production was not the order of the day as I am afraid it is today in many dramatic academies. For instance, Mr. Fisher White who produced us in Shakespeare scenes in the 'theatre' found time to instruct us in the Emil Behnke system of voice production. It was not his job, but as there was no established voice production class he gave us his expert knowledge of the art as he learned it from Hermann Vezin and Kate Emil Behnke.

Often during rehearsals at His Majesty's, Mr. Tree would turn to Fisher White for guidance when he wanted to speak a longish sentence in one breath. Tree was envious of White's control of voice and body. Mrs. Kate Crowe, née Bateman, a wonderful link with Irving and the great days at the Lyceum, took us in classroom Shakespeare, long speeches and duologues, fiercely correcting the diction and demanding poise. Her description of Irving as an actor held us enthralled, her opinion of him as a man was not flattering. A short, stumpy woman, a hooked nose and eyes with the glint of a hawk, a carriage that reminded one that she had been Lady Macbeth to Irving's Macbeth and had pulled the Town as Leah. She always carried a stick and if displeased, poked you with it as she explained what she wanted.

As a titbit for being a good boy she prepared me as Henry V in the wooing scene which I played at a church charity function with her niece Leah Bateman as the Princess. I was the envy of the male students.

During my first term Fred Kerr was persuaded by Tree to rehearse us in the Pinero farces. I say persuaded because Kerr did not believe in a school of acting. He was famous as a comedian in the modern plays of the age. His performances of irascible aristocrats were a feature of many productions and gossip told us that he was irascible and aristocratic off as on stage, a snob, judging people by their clothes and education. Poor me with my poor wardrobe and 3d per week education! We all I think, I certainly, awaited his appearance with apprehension.

He was ushered into the theatre room by the administrator Mr. George Bancroft who, emulating his famous father Sir Squire, was always sartorially effective, but Fred Kerr outshone him. Black and white check trousers, black coat and vest, heavily braided stock tie with a magnificent pin, Edward VII homburg, doeskin gloves, a gold knobbed cane and spats. Not very tall, rather round shouldered, a chubby face and a snub nose. He chainsmoked cigars. After announcing that Mr. Kerr would rehearse us in Mr. Pinero's *The Times* and reading the cast, Mr. Bancroft left us. I was cast for the clergyman.

Mr. Kerr eyed us aggressively, swung a chair round, sat astride, leaning over the back. 'You wish to become actors and actresses,' he said with a grumbling voice—'well God help you, God help you, anyway, I'll do what I can.' In the early stages of the first lesson the balloon went up. A student welcoming a character named Montague pronounced it Montag. 'Oh my God,' growled Kerr, 'Monta<u>gue</u>, Monta<u>gue</u>, where the hell have you been dragged up.' The student, trembling with fear, in fact we were all atremble, repeated the sentence and in his anxiety spat out the few false teeth he was wearing. 'God help me,' shouted Kerr, 'Now he spits his teeth out, God help the profession.' We were dumb with fear, he stared at us and then gave vent to long belly laugh through which he said, 'Never mind, old son, I saw that happen to Lionel Brough during a performance.' Aristocrat and snob, but the laugh was behind all the biting criticism we suffered.

Kerr was an actor of the naturalistic school, disliking the cloak and dagger drama and with no time for Shakespeare. Any movement or utterance that was not absolutely natural made him writhe, and he rehearsed an offending move or sentence a hundred times and then we began to see daylight. A spontaneous effort delighted him and I won his approval by my attack on my clergyman role. To my delight he reported his pleasure to the administrator.

The oft repeated question—if some of the artists of the past were with us today . . . ? If Fred Kerr could return, he would take his place in the front rank in modern comedy. At any rehearsal we saw him through a haze of cigar smoke. During my period at the Academy Lyall Swete guided us through the intricacies of Browning's *Blot in the 'Scutcheon*, *In a Balcony*, and Robertson's *School*. Sir Squire and Lady Bancroft sometimes looked in during rehearsals of the latter.

Swete, with his heavy body and high pitched voice, was on the whole as gentle as Kerr was rough, but he could lose his temper and then he behaved like a woman. Kerr in his tantrums frightened us, Swete made us laugh. How he loved his Browning and caressed us through the many passages we did not understand. Then as now female students outnumbered the men and I cannot remember how many Mildreds and Treshams were in the *Blot* or how many ladies listened to me as Norbert in the *Balcony*.

I don't know whether Swete summed me up but Tresham was type casting. I was a very staid young man, my puritanical upbringing was strong within me and caused many of my fellow students to call me Daddy, so I was ripe for upholding the Treshams' dignity when Mildred made the blot.

The action of Swete was invaluable, he insisted on long passages being spoken on one breath and would earmark the passages and hand us over to the deep-breathing lady for practice. Fisher White confined himself to Shakespeare and the reading of poetry. A lovable man, heart and soul behind Tree's experiment. A fine face and voice, a complete master of stage technique. An ideal tutor. To his sorrow he was short in stature and he often cursed nature for robbing him of the inches that prevented him from becoming a leading man. I owe him much. So did Tree, for often during rehearsals at His Majesty's he would appeal to Fisher White for technical guidance and then the little man would assume the port of Mars and in illustrating Tree's requirements he appeared to be 6′ 1″ to his chief's 6′. Tree's admiration for White's accomplishments was tinged with envy and he often pulled his leg maliciously. Tree was a master of make-up, using very few sticks of grease paint and effecting his disguise within ten minutes or so. White used water colours, as Irving did, spending two hours to effect the change. During breaks at rehearsal Tree loved to gossip with his company and on one occasion the subject of make-up cropped up. 'Yes,' said Tree, his baleful eyes fixed upon White, 'take Mr. Fisher White for instance. He reminds me of Sir Henry Irving who each night at 6 o'clock pushed his key into his private entrance of the Lyceum, entered his dressing room and emerged upon the Lyceum stage at 8.30 looking exactly as he did at 6 p.m.'

But to return to the Academy. A dominant figure was Madam Cavalazzi, Mistress of the Mime, a one-time ballerina, a fiery Italian. Under her we lived, loved and died in every possible posture. Her comic use of the English language gave us many a laugh. After an exercise she would go up to a

In 1905 I was thrilled by my first opera which I saw from the slips at Covent Garden, *Madam Butterfly* with Caruso and Destinn singing. My early longings for a musical career were revived, but alas there was no musical side at the Academy. Tree invited the school to see the final dress rehearsal of his production of *Oliver Twist*, adapted by J. Comyns Carr. This was an exciting event as two of our fellow students were playing parts. Reginald Owen, now a feature player in Hollywood, was Tom Chitling, and Yates Southgate, Giles the butler to Mrs. Maylie. How we envied them. During an interval we were regaled with sandwiches and coffee in the dress circle bar and Mr. Tree, as Fagin, came and said how do you do to us. What a Fagin he was and who ever saw the performance will I am sure never forgot the greatness of Lyn Harding and Constance Collier as Sykes and Nancy.

During my second term I greatly missed James Fernandez and his warm hearted encouragement. The gap was filled by none other than the great George Alexander, who rehearsed us in Pinero's *The Profligate*. He was the social bug of the St. James's, very stiff and starchy. He rehearsed us as from a social distance. I played the part originally written for Forbes-Robertson. We never warmed to G.A. nor he to us. One good thing he did was to take some rehearsals at the St. James's Theatre; after the cramped conditions at 62 it was tremendously helpful and even G.A. thawed a bit.

Was G.A. a very good actor? In 1907 I saw him in *The Thief*, a play adapted from the French by Cosmo Gordon-Lennox. Later I saw Lucien Guitry and his French company perform the play. G.A. was very inferior to Guitry. What a great actor this Frenchman was! His Pasteur was a performance that lives in the memory.

But Alexander's reign at the St. James's was a notable page in theatrical history—apart from setting many fashions for men's neckwear. He surrounded himself with fine talent, artists and playwrights including Oscar Wilde, Stephen Phillips and Pinero. He introduced the golden voiced Harry Ainley to London, and Ainley's 'Paolo' in Phillips' *Paolo and Francesca* drew all London to Society's theatre in King Street. At one rehearsal of *The Profligate* at the St. James's, we suffered a terrifying experience. Pinero came in and took over from G.A. I suppose Pinero was the first author producer. We had heard of the severe manner he adopted towards his casts, his rudeness to the stars and how they quailed before him. Even Mrs. Patrick Campbell had to obey him. His 'good afternoon, ladies and gentlemen' was replied to by nervous bows and weak voices.

He listened to a scene, I say listened because during the action he walked up and down the stalls gangway with bent head, his gloved hands clasped behind him. He wore a black suit, hat and overcoat. During his perambulations one anticipated he would disappear at any moment—

24

in disgust—but no, at the conclusion of the scene he gazed at us for a moment, disappeared through the pass door and came on to the stage. His walk was firm, but very precise. He took off his hat and right hand glove, placed them with meticulous care upon a table. Of medium height, an almond shaped face, very bald, eyes that looked through you, and eyebrows ebony black that seemed to jut out inches, each hair seemed to be like thin wire. From his overcoat pocket he produced a bound copy of the play, this was held firmly during the course of instruction in his calf-gloved hand. The right hand hung a little behind his back, without touching the body, and waggled incessantly and very vigorously when driving home a point. He was not concerned with our movements. The words were his interest and as each character spoke he advanced upon the player and we stood toe to toe. Each sentence was built up word by word, the book would tap the player's chin to point a rhythm, the eyebrows would scratch the forehead as voice and eyes simulated an inflection, an intonation, tempo into a reeling brain. 'Articulation,' he would hiss, 'the theatre is not a drawing room.' This scorching examination of our qualities left us exhausted, but Mr. Pinero beamed upon us, and turning to G.A. said 'Not a bad bunch, Alec. Good bye, I will see you again.' G.A. explained that when Mr. P. came to the first rehearsal of a new play he knew exactly what he wanted from every artist and was adamant toward a professional cast to that end, as he had treated us he treated the professionals, stars and all, it was a compliment to us and to him, G.A., that he stayed as long.

During my second term the administrator sent for me to tell me that the following term might offer possibilities of a far-reaching nature. This worried me, again I had no money for a third term. I did not want to appeal to Mr. Bancroft again and I doubted if the Luton folk would stump up again. To Uncle I was wasting my time, I was not earning money.

One day, glancing through the *Era*, the theatrical paper of the day, I noticed an advertisement offering a 'Punch and Judy Show'. My Punch and Judy Show was still intact at Luton. I wrote to my Luton friend Mrs. Walshe and through her help (having arranged to spend the Christmas vacation at my Luton home) trotted my Punch and Judy Show to children's homes and Christmas parties in the district, picking up 5/-, 10/- and £1 per performance. Thus I assured myself of a third term. On telling Mr. Bancroft of my Christmas activities, he said, 'that's fine, it shows guts'.

The third term opened in January 1906 and I was greeted with momentous news. I was among the students chosen to walk on in Mr. Tree's production of *Nero* opening 26 January 1906, and I was to play 'Shylock' in the trial scene from the *Merchant of Venice* and the Old Pierrot in the wordless play *L'Enfant Prodigue* in a programme of scenes to be played by the students at His Majesty's Theatre in aid of the G. R. Sims 'Referee' children's fund.

Attending rehearsals at the theatre and classes at 62 made up a full week and made heavy inroads into my weekly 7/- for living. However, 'Henny', Mrs. Henderson, who ran the canteen in the basement of 62, kept an eye on the not too well-to-dos and provided nourishing titbits on the side. No persons in the world prayed for my success more than this ample bodied and large hearted woman and her husband, the sergeant on the door.

I was a rather serious young man, my puritan upbringing still guided thought and action and, attractive as the opposite sex was to me—off stage—my behaviour towards them was decorum personified. I was often shocked by the worldly utterances of some of my fellow students, and there was many a laugh at my expense. I was really very popular and one and all predicted a successful career. I suppose I presented a one-track mind. This belief in me generated a confidence denied me by the, I suppose, lovable browbeating during my boyhood. Deep friendships were made, one in particular, David Powell and myself were inseparable, we were known as David and Jonathan. He too was a Welshman and provided the first romance of the 1905 term, falling in love with a beautiful dark lady of the Academy. David had no inhibitions and in confidence beguiled me with the progress of his courtship. I was not jealous or envious, no I was analytical and picked up many titbits for building up a love scene, on the stage. In return for his confidence I demanded his pound of flesh for he was Antonio to my Shylock in the students' matinee.

Classes were fitted in during the rehearsal period for *Nero* and how proud we felt telling the students who were not included in the production. 'Yes, I am just going to' or 'have just come from rehearsal'. A thrilling moment too, on being summoned to Mr. Dana's office to sign one's contract. Twenty eight shillings a week. I was a minor but allowed to sign on my own behalf. Mr. Henry Dana, Mr. Tree's general manager and watchdog, a thin pale man with a moustache that shouted efficiency, welcomed us with a wan smile and hoped we would be happy and bring honour to Mr. Tree's experiment.

Before the first rehearsal Mr. Cecil King, the stage manager, read a kind of riot act as to our behaviour. Punctuality, to keep out of the way when not wanted on the set during rehearsals, no smoking, no watching in the wings, and during the run to remain in our dressing room when not occupied on the stage, to obey the call boy and not to wander along the ladies' corridors—if found doing so without permission, instant dismissal. C.K. was rough and rude, we seemed to be intruders and the overtone was, 'A school of acting, I'll school 'em.' The call boy was Claude Rains—now a Hollywood star—a friendly boy and although petted by the leading members of the cast, he hobnobbed with us and we soon discovered that he too had made up his mind to become a star actor. Even then, with a slight cockney accent and diminutive stature, he possessed a dominating personality.

At the first rehearsal of *Nero*, Mr. Tree welcomed each one of his pupils with a handshake and as we walked away he glanced at his company with eyes that seemed to say 'Oh! dear, what have I done.' He was ignorant of our qualities because during my two terms we had seen little or nothing of him.

From our retreat at the back of the stage I gazed with excitement mixed with awe at the players. Lyn Harding, Basil Gill, C. W. Somerset, Esmé Percy, Mrs. Tree, Constance Collier and Dorothea Baird, the famous Trilby, and of course our tutor, Fisher White.

I was cast as a Roman gentleman who cheered Nero in the street and in the banquet scene dallied with a lady upon a divan and between the dallies and ordered interest in the scene ate grapes and drank wine—cold tea. To my regret I have forgotten the name of my lady. There was a dignity and discipline at the opening of morning rehearsal. The company would assemble five minutes before the scheduled time and on the dot Mr. Tree, having breakfasted in his Dome apartment at the top of the building, would enter through the swing doors of the stage ceremoniously opened by Mr. King, and bow to the company as he advanced to the centre.

There was an almost click of the heels as the gentlemen said 'Good morning sir,' one or two said chief, but the sobriquet still belonged to the late Sir Henry Irving. Mrs. Tree would advance and claim her morning kiss—she did not share the Dome with him—and Miss Collier and Miss Baird would receive attention. Sometimes he had not finished his breakfast by rehearsal time, then he would appear, egg and spoon in hand, followed by his valet with a tray bearing coffee and bread and butter. This did not interfere with the ritual and rehearsal would begin as he finished his repast.

The rehearsal period held many exciting incidents. Attendance at the costumiers B. J. Simmons & Co., where during the fittings, fat, tall, sandy haired Mr. Simmons shouted at short, angel faced Mr. Rossi, the cutter, and Mr. Rossi shouted at Mr. Simmons. These verbal duels were less terrifying when Mr. Percy Macquoid, the designer, was present, giving as much delicate attention to my yellow tunic and cloak as if I was Mr. Tree himself. And then to Wardour Street to be welcomed by the world famous perruquier Willie Clarkson, who calling for Gus Rogers introduced us as 'the gentlemen from Mr. Tree's Academy, and please, Mr. Rogers, give as much attention to

The final calls produced pandemonium, the audience on their feet waving everything they could get hold of and the crush against the orchestra barrier made one fear for its stability. Miss Terry insisted upon the full company, stage staff and all being upon the stage, and during one curtain drop she turned to Mr. Tree saying, 'Herbert, I hope some of this is for Henry.' The Terry excitement and watching Tree revive six of his great performances made my Shakespearean baptism a week of wonder.

The resumption of the run of *Nero* returned me to the state of supernumerary, but not for long for Michael Morton's *Colonel Newcome*, an adaptation of Thackeray's *The Newcomes*, was put into rehearsal and I was cast for Bowkins, the leader of the deputation asking Colonel Newcome to stand for Parliament, plus a guest in the ballroom scene and a pensioner of Grey Friars Hospital, aged 90.

The script of the roles, Bowkins a few lines, the guest none and the pensioner one word, 'Adsum', was handed to me the day before the first rehearsal. To my stupefaction Bowkins was labelled 'dialect' and I had no knowledge of any dialect. No. 62 had not enlightened me in that branch of the art of acting. However my newly found friend from the cast of *Nero*, Esmond Egerton Hine, not a product of the Academy, possessed a copy of the Book and we eagerly searched the pages for the history of Bowkins, without success, but we gathered enough to agree that this fictitious character came from South Bedfordshire. As a boy I had listened to a careless use of the English language, the consonant being sacred, without being personally affected, and I thought I would try it out with Bowkins.

After the first rehearsal of the scene, Mr. Tree, who I don't believe had read the book, gestured me to his side and asked what dialect I was using. South Bedfordshire, I tremorously replied, anticipating the snatching of the part from my hand, but no, 'Ah yes, Ah yes,' he said, and then with a dubious look, 'Keep it in.'

Collins' Clear-Type Press issued a new edition of the *The Newcomes* coinciding with the production of *Colonel Newcome* and among others I am represented by a full-page photograph in my character, but the name Bowkins does not appear. The adaptors added a few 'Adsums' to Thackeray, the final scene being a roll call and exit of the pensioners, mine being the penultimate squeak, leaving Mr. Tree to say 'Adsum', and then die.

In 1917, Sir Herbert, as he was then, appeared as Colonel Newcome in New York in his last performance of an American tour. 'Adsum' was the last word he spoke upon a stage for within a few weeks of his return to England he died.

If Sir Herbert could come back from the year 1906 and play Col. Newcome he would be hailed as a great actor, for he took Thomas Newcome from the pages of Thackeray and placed him on the stage. In that memorable production I came under the spell of Marion Terry, and (Oh! how pretty she was) Marie Lohr. Lillian Braithwaite played Ethel Newcome and the old war horse from No. 62, Mrs. Kate Crowe, 'Lady Kew'. She expressed her delight with my progress. The production was marred by an untoward incident. A few days before the opening night, a London 'daily' published an anonymous scurrilous article demanding Tree should not appear as Col. Newcome. It attacked his origin, his legs, his guttural accent; how dare he attempt to appear as a grand old English gentleman? Gossip was rife as to the author, many names were mentioned, theatrical, literary, and journalistic, but the person of spite lay doggo. The damage was done—the first night saw few people waiting in the pit and gallery queues.

I well remember the rehearsal on the day the article appeared: from the flymen downward, all vowed vengeance upon the perpetrator when he was discovered. One learned that heaven and earth were being moved to drag his name from the offending newspaper's office.

Mr. Tree visibly suffered under the smart and it needed the help of his friend Comyns Carr at rehearsals to regain confidence—this he did and on the first night he was inspired and packed stalls and circle gave him an ovation. The play ran from 29 May to 7 July, a short run for H.M.T.; the poison had done its work. Some years later I met a playwright, a handsome and most charming man; we met many times, over meals, at a club, in bars, exchanging ideas and talking about the past. He died in 1939. It was after then that I learned that he was the author of the vicious article—for why? Money; he died an extremely rich gentleman. Col. Newcome brought to an end my first season at H.M.T.

First impressions are always wonderful. Well, my first impression of my first master was, what a wonderful man. I met many wonderful people and saw many wonderful performances. It was all wonderful—it still is.

The autumn programme, as announced by Mr. Tree on the last night, was for him and his company a short provincial tour of revivals during which *Antony and Cleopatra* would be prepared for London and his presentation at H.M.T. of *The Winter's Tale* with Ellen Terry as Hermione, Mrs. Tree Paulina, Viola Tree Perdita, Charles Warner as Leontes and C. W. Somerset Autolycus. Tree at times used strange means to convey news that might be displeasing to another person. He was childishly cowardly at times, morally and physically. As an instance I will relate a story told to me by Lyn Harding as near as I can remember it in Harding's own words.

Tree wanted me to play Polixenes in his 1906 revival of *The Winter's Tale*. I wasn't keen on the part, but asked who would be the Leontes.

Quizzing me with a look that suggested I was after the lead he proudly said Johnstone Forbes-Robertson will play Leontes. Oh, I replied, that's a wonderful idea and hastily added that I could play Camillo because it would be a thrilling experience to play the Camillo scene with Forbie. Tree agreed, and I made the further suggestion that my contract should contain the words. Forbes-Robertson will play Leontes. Tree agreed to this and the contract duly arrived containing those lines. A week or so later during a matinee of *Col. Newcome*, Tree asked me to supper in the Dome that night. Oh I said, I came up from Enfield today in my gardening clothes. I'm not fit to appear in the Dome, thinking of course it was to be a party affair. Oh, said Tree, your clothes won't worry me, it's only we two, a nice little chat, good food I hope, you know the wine will be good and a cigar. By the time his man had cleared the table leaving us with the brandy and cigars I began to wonder why he had kept me from my bed for we had talked about nothing that mattered and he seemed very uneasy—incidentally we were both pretty tight. At 3 o'clock when I was very tight and angry and he was tight and very vague he suddenly said, I am going to bed, and pulling his bed down from the wall he began to undress and when he had donned his pyjamas disappeared into the bathroom. I wanted to smash the place up. He returned, got into bed, and turning his back on me said. 'You know your way out'. In a fury I rushed to the door and as I was opening it he called me back. I turned, he had turned, and with his head peeping under the sheet said, 'Charles Warner will play Leontes, you know how to use the lift. Good night, dear Lyn, and oh please switch off the lights.'

Before leaving London to spend part of the vacation at Luton, I saw Pinero's play *His House in Order* at the St. James's Theatre. This play is still to me one of the best plays in the English language. Of its time it was true to life. Its success boded such a long London run that George Alexander, seeing little chance of touring himself, personally directed two companies for the provinces.

The provinces were nursed in those days: the London success was played by a touring company without the personal supervision of the London manager. Also the average provincial theatre was a more comfortable place than it is today—they were individual and well managed. To Lord's I went, for the first time, to watch the Gentlemen and Players. The players entered the field from the side door; I saw Rhodes, Hayward, Lillie and Tyldesley. To Luton I proudly bore the news that in Mr. Tree's autumn tour I was to play the Bishop of Carlisle in *Richard II*, the Colonel in *The Man Who Was* and the lawyer in *Business is Business*. My elevation to the

Bishop and the Colonel was because Fisher White was to be Antigonus—in *The Winter's Tale* at H.M.T. I had stepped into my tutor's shoes. My aunt, not knowing exactly what it all meant, was overjoyed at my seeming success. Uncle was inwardly pleased, but outraged that I was to receive no money during the closed season; but on presenting myself to Mr. J. C. Kershaw, of Kershaw & Co., straw hat manufacturer and plait merchants, I was a hero and was presented with a boater, straight from the block.

Many rehearsals for the 1906 autumn tour took place in the dress circle bar of H.M.T. as the stage was occupied by the *Winter's Tale* company; whenever possible myself and others watched from the back of the Circle, Miss Ellen Terry rehearsing Hermione. 'She is too old,' I heard whispered around me, 'she is too old.' Was she? I did not know, anyway, who was I to pass judgement?

How often since, when addressing students I have said, 'Do not criticise famous elders; criticise yourselves and attain their position.' My memory from the back of that circle is of a voice of unbelievable beauty and a grace of movement, in spite of an inclination to stoutness.

The method of production was persuasive: 'Herbert,' (Mr. Tree directing) 'here, I would like to do this'; 'Charles dear,' (Warner), 'could you be a little nearer to me?'—'Don't be stiff, Julius, don't be stiff'—this to Julius Knight, an Australian actor, playing Polixenes, his first appearance in England. Even I had to agree with Miss Terry, he was stiff—a fine figure of a man and handsome but he acted and spoke as one might suppose Charles Kemble did.

From the back of that circle I first saw O. B. Clarence, rehearsing the 'young shepherd'; it was many years after that I met him. Charles Warner, famous for his fine performance and spectacular death fall from a high scaffolding in the play *Drink* from the French *L'Assommoir*, was what was known as an intense actor.

During a rehearsal of the statue scene, Warner, moving towards Miss Terry, suddenly stopped and with tremendous dignity said, 'Nell, I beg you don't, don't do it, Nell.' We didn't know till later what Nell was doing. Under emotion, Warner would clench his right hand leaving the thumb sticking up and as emotion waxed, the thumb waggled. This amused Miss Terry, who, sotto voce, would say to the standers-by on the scene, 'Oh look at his thumb, look at his thumb; Oh! somebody lasso it.' She was very naughty at times; once, standing near her in the wings during the *Merry Wives*, she loudly commented upon Viola Tree who, as Nan Page, was playing a scene with Fenton, 'Charming girl, charming, put her into a spotted dress and she would look like a figure from a Botticelli—delicious creature—pity she can't act.'

41

The members of the touring company were invited to the first night of the *Winter's Tale*, and apart from Miss Terry my main remembrance is the realistic beauty of the pastoral scene, complete with cottage and cascading brook, in the waters of which C. W. Somerset, as Autolycus, washed his hands and face as he trilled 'When daffodils begin to peer' etc. I believe that thousands of playgoers of today would applaud that sample of Tree's artistic realism. His answer to Florizel's 'What have we twain forgot?' was the disappearance of the two lovers and their re-appearance with the pet dove in a wicker cage. The tour produced a disappointment: *Richard II* was dropped from the repertoire, this after all the care, under the guidance of Fisher White, I had given to the study of the Bishop of Carlisle. During the vacation the leaves of the hedgerows of the Luton countryside had quivered under the power of my

> Prevent, resist it, let it not be so,
> Lest children's children cry against you 'Noe'

But my chance with the role was to come. Anyway Mr. Tree had provided liberally for me. My original part in *Col. Newcome*, the lawyer in *Business is Business*, Dr. Oliver in *Trilby*, the Royal Barber in *The Ballad Monger* and Col. Durgan in *The Man Who Was*.

It is strange as I look back to think that a youth of twenty years, a humble member of a company of stars and such notable players as Edmund Maurice, G. W. Anson, 'Bobby' Brough, the son of Lionel, Charles Quartermaine, A. E. Benedict, son of the composer, should be cast not only as a Colonel of the White Hussars, but the husband of Constance Collier. Anyway Mr. Tree's faith in me caused the critic of the *Birmingham Gazette*, 24 October 1906, to write:

> Miss Constance Collier as Millicent Durgan is good and Mr. R. Atkins as Colonel Durgan notably so.

The *Liverpool Post*, referring to my performance in the *Ballad Monger*, printed:

> Mr. Robert Atkins as the 'ennobled' Royal barber added to the conventionality of a stage villain, a good delivery and much facility of facial expression.

So my name was in the papers.

The poison of the London papers' attack on Tree's production of *Col. Newcome* was echoed in a Birmingham daily prior to the performance of Tuesday 24 October 1906, and after the Wednesday performance of *The Man Who Was* Tree addressed the audience, backed up by Marie Corelli. The stumpy little lady stamped and gesticulated, shouted, attacking the press in general for their attack upon the production. I'm sure that the Flowers of Stratford on Avon, whose arch enemy she was, never experienced the scorn of her tongue as did the Birmingham press that night.

Tree, dressed in the rags of Austin Limmason, said:

'You see I come to you in sack-cloth and ashes, I have an apology—or as they say in another place—a personal explanation to make. When I bought the Birmingham papers today I was surprised at the divergence of opinion upon the presentation of *Col. Newcome* last night. We are often over-praised and sometimes unduly blamed—we are not so black or so white as we are painted—we are more often grey. But I feel I have been worrying today for a newspaper which has a deservedly high reputation not only here in Birmingham, but elsewhere in the kingdom also has accused me of presenting to you an unworthy play. It is called an outrage, an annoyance, the veriest rubbish, a vulgarisation, an outrage upon Thackeray; it is like fifth rate claret; it is marring and debasing; it is crude and clumsy; its language so like a halfpenny novelette; and it is a mere caricature.
I hope I may claim not to be guilty of presenting such a work to the Birmingham public. I may at least claim that it was reverently done, and as Shakespeare says, "Nothing can offend when simpleness and duty tender it."
And now I may tell you in face of this wholesale condemnation that the production referred to has received the unstinted approval of the late novelist's family and that Mr. Thackeray's distinguished daughter, Mrs. Richmond Ritchie, wrote me a most delightful letter, in which she said "My father often wondered if the creation of the brain could one day come into actual being. I am sorry he was not here tonight to see his speculation verified." '

The speech, delivered with great humility, was responded to by vehement applause. One paper, reporting the curtain fall demonstration, suggested that Miss Corelli must have come straight from London, where the day before "raucous women" had raided the Lords and the Commons, demanding the vote. Theatrical touring fifty years ago was a far happier affair than it is today, for then there seemed to be in every touring date a bunch of land-ladies who made it their business to make the weekly visit of the 'troupe' as happy and comfortable as the accommodation they had to offer would allow.

There were exceptions, and these were duly noted in the book of signatures, laid open upon the breakfast table, on the Sunday morning of departure, with a penny bottle of Stevens ink and pen to hand. Eulogists' insertions, such as 'A home from home', 'mother's cooking', 'will always return' were common, but now and again one noted, 'Quoth the Raven ... ...' leaving the landlady to fill in the missing words.

These accommodating families were confined to a street or series of streets in a certain district. Two spring to my mind, Bath Row, Birmingham and Ackers Street, Manchester, the latter being a standing joke for many music-hall comedians of the day. On the first tour, to keep expenses down, I shared digs with Henry Hewitt and Sam Warmington. Our requirements were a sitting room and double and single bedrooms, taking weekly turns to enjoy the single bed. At times we had to share a bedroom for three.

Henry was the business manager, a canny fellow, and woe betide the landlady if we had to stump up more than fifteen shillings per week each. On the whole we fared well, a happy trio. The lodging streets that met the measure of our purses usually presented a long unbroken facade of flat faced houses with the universal aspidistra peering through the parlour windows. More often than not the sitting room offered held a touch of theatricality by being wallpapered a deep fading red with black horizontal lines and golden devices dotted about. Invariably the mantlepiece was surmounted by a large scale mirror with a gold frame. The centre table when not engaged for meals sported a red or green plush cloth with a tassled fringe. There was always a picture to remind one of the heroic past such as *The Thin Red Line* or *Kitchener at Khartoum* and always framed in walnut. The bedrooms were often gaily papered, trellis work with roses being a favourite theme, the bedsteads were iron with brass knobs and the floor covering always linoleum. Bathrooms were scarce, and when available were sometimes crude set-ups. I remember one at Hull that had naked gas jets under the bath to heat the water. I remember it well for on the Monday morning I forgot to obey the landlady's instructions to turn the jets off before getting in, and burnt my behind.

In subsequent towns my salary allowed me to climb the social ladder and seek apartments in bow-windowed terraces with front doors that boasted panels of stained glass. By and large these large-hearted hard-working women eking out their hardworking husbands' weekly pittance by their care for the pros were proud of a favourable entry in the book of signatures. Many are the tales of those far away touring days. An item at the foot of one weekly bill read 'cruet 3/6', this cruet took a journey to the next town. Then there was the landlady who placed a bunch of asparagus in a vase hoping that the stems would flower before the end of the week, and another who served Benger's food as porridge.

As in London, Tree had taken Irving's place in the provincial cities and large towns, the tour was in the nature of a royal progress. It was progress for me too for I was seeing England for the first time, and being 'on the road'

44

gave me a sense of being a 'laddie'. Laddie and Cully were terms still in use to denote the actor. Our arrival at Blackpool provided a shock. A horse-drawn char-a-banc awaited the company for the purpose of conveying them to their lodgings, the sides bearing streamers stating that 'Herbert Beerbohm Tree has arrived'. On the front seats were two men, one with a big drum and the other flourishing a coaching horn. This form of circus transit was not accepted by 'His Majesty's Theatre Co.'. We learned that Mr. Tree was displeased with the local manager's approach to advertising.

We entertained Manchester for two weeks at the Theatre Royal, now a cinema. Mr. John Hare was at the Prince's, playing *A Pair of Spectacles* and *Caste*. The old Queen's was run by Mr. Flanagan, who, following the tradition of the Calverts, delighted Mancunians with an annual spectacular production of a Shakespeare play. Miss Nora Lancaster, our juvenile lead, had made a tremendous hit in the spring of 1906 with her performance of Rosalind at the Queen's and her description of the scenic realism gives an idea of Flanagan's approach to Shakespearean production.

> When the curtain rose on the Forest of Arden the realism of the mighty poles and twisting branches, foliage, grass, hummocks and rivulets, wild flowers galore was added to by the appearance of six deer and twelve rabbits—the animals could only walk or hop a certain distance because they were tethered off stage.
> The audience would applaud the scene, then the animals, then Mr. Flanagan, who at matinees in morning suit with silk hat, at night in full evening dress with silk hat, would proudly bow to audience and animals as the curtain fell. A few minutes later, the animals being retired from the scene, the curtain would rise again and the play allowed to proceed.

Business is Business, Sydney Grundy's adaptation from the French of *Les Affaires sont les Affaires*, was new to the provinces and Mr Tree's performance of the Jewish financier Isadore Izard found more favour than London bestowed upon it. One up for the provinces, for this was indeed a very great piece of acting showing humour and tragedy. My part in the play was that of a shady lawyer, watching the interests of a pilsener-loving German, beautifully played by G. W. Anson, doing business with the Jew. My lines were not plentiful but the stage business introduced into the one scene in which my part appeared was very intricate, sly glances, warning gestures, laughter, incurring sounding thumps on the back from Izard and through it all making myself look lazy with a very large cigar. Everything about Izard was large, including the new ruin he had caused to be built in his large grounds.

It was a truly wonderful experience for a young actor to rehearse and play such a scene with H. B. Tree and G. W. Anson, and one had to be on one's mettle for Tree was a man of moods on the stage and one had to be ready to react to the new tone of a line, or a movement that had not been rehearsed.

G. W. Anson, newly returned from a long and successful season in Australia, was up to all the tricks and gave me many tips on timing and listening. In *Business is Business* I felt for the first time that I really mattered. I felt I was getting somewhere. Kinsey Peile's one act characterisation of Kipling's story *The Man Who Was* was a magnificent vehicle for Tree's tour de force as Austin Limmason. It was billed with *Business is Business* and I am sure that two more remarkable contrasts in characterisation have seldom been placed in juxtaposition in a single evening's bill.

Tree as a producer was ninety per cent right; as an actor he was not technically over-equipped, but he possessed the gift of identification, sometimes with a terrifying insight. This quality made him such an interesting and at times an alarming person to act with for from performance to performance one never knew what changes would creep into his characterisation, but whatever the changes they were always within the 'character'. A virtue of his method was that those acting with him seldom became stereotyped. To have seen him turned from the bloated common humorous and tragic Jewish financier to the mute groping bag of bones of the *Man Who Was* is a thrilling remembrance.

My share in the double bill was useful, for to pass from the suave craftiness of the lawyer to the dignity of Colonel Durgan was an exercise in versatility. I was really too young for Durgan, but my serious demeanour, plus an iron grey wig and being well coached by Fisher White, helped me to tear off a performance.

Dublin gave *The Man Who Was* a hot reception. We had been warned of a possible disturbance but were not prepared for the clamour that greeted the playing of the National Anthem by the regimental band of the White Hussars before the curtain rose and showed the Officers Mess and their guests standing with upraised glasses waiting for me to speak the opening line, 'The Queen, God bless her'. Victoria, of course. I was really frightened and uncertain whether to speak, but Edmund Maurice, the (Russian guest Dirkovitch) caught my eye and prompted me to 'hold it'. By this time the mess larder was added to by a considerable supply of vegetables. These came from the upper reaches of the house, and the stalls and pit joined in the uproar, peaceful Dubliners attempting to quieten the anti-Royalists. The curtain was rung down, and after an appeal by the manager of the theatre, for Dublin to sustain the honour of Dublin, and after the free gifts of produce had been collected (the stage staff did well that night) the play proceeded without a repetition of the anthem or the spoken lines for the Toast. The reception at the end was tremendous, The Phoenix Parkites had had their say and as far as they were concerned honours were even.

That was my first experience of the 'Bird', although the Dublin biped was a politcal not a theatrical one. 'What Manchester says today London will say tomorrow' is theatrically more true today than it was in 1906. But Tree did ask Manchester, in 1895, to pass judgement upon his production of *Trilby* before London saw him as Svengali with Dorothea Baird as Trilby. The 1906 tour introduced Miss Constance Collier to the provinces in the title role. What a lovely person she was both in looks and nature, and her Trilby, my first, was to me a beautiful performance. I had a tiny scene with her as Dr. Oliver and how lovingly she helped me with the words and movements. 'Ah!' said the wise heads of the Manchester Arts Club, the hospitality of which had been extended to the males of our company, 'You should have seen Dorothea Baird in the part.' Twas ever thus and while a theatre exists the words, 'You should have seen' will echo down the ages, but gentle readers, 'You should have seen' Tree as Svengali. Since he 'shook off this mortal coil' I have seen many gifted actors attempt the part, but all have paled beside the character that Tree placed before his public.

My honorary membership of the Manchester Arts Club introduced me to clubland and my frequent but shy visits helped me to gain an assurance when meeting people not earning their living in the theatre and certainly with more erudition than I possessed.

Do I remember a vision of James Agate, in rather sporty attire? He did not speak to me personally but I am sure it was from him that the room heard what Montague had said that morning in the *Guardian*. And then from, I think it was a Mr. Sladen, I learned of the perfectness of the Hallé Orchestra, and listened to stories of Hans Richter as a conductor. During the tour, in duty bound, I visited art galleries, museums and points of historical interest. My room mates were not keen on this form of mental recreation, but Warmington, who had a smattering knowledge of literature, was responsible for my first serious, if at the time perfunctory, study of Shakespeare. Dear, 70 year old Mrs. E. H. Brooke took a motherly interest in my welfare and often invited me to take tea with her, and her stories of the glories of the past always led to her husband's performance of Iago. Even Irving's paled beside it. Iago always entered after the tea and cakes, and the little lady rising from her throne—yes, that Victorian armchair became a throne as she sat in it, reminding one of Queen Victoria, dressed as she was in black and wearing a black bonnet trimmed with black lace—taking the floor would instruct me in the salient points of her husband's performance, imitating his gestures and vocal tones.

One moment I well remember: 'And at this point, to speak the line "But let her live," my husband moved back, speaking the line from behind Othello's left ear; the audience heard the voice of an angel, and saw the face of a devil.' I had never seen a performance of *Othello* and was not too conversant with the play, but when it was my lot to tackle the role of Iago, that moment of description was my yardstick.

Revealing my teatime experience to Warmington, he sarcastically suggested my becoming acquainted with the lectures of A. C. Bradley. The 1905 edition was then on sale and I purchased a copy. So I began to dabble in a serious study of the four great Tragedies. I say dabble because I found the lectures heavy going and I was putting the cart before the horse, not having studied the text of the plays. I had seen F. R. Benson and H. B. Irving play Hamlet, and had supported Mr. Tree as Marcellus, but I could not reconcile any of these performances with the profundities of Bradley. Lear and Macbeth I put on one side, played with the more familiar text of *Hamlet*, but really struggled to get inside *Othello*, making Iago the leading role.

When in 1908, at Shrewsbury, I first appeared as Iago with the Benson North Company, my study of the role was a mixture of Brooke and Bradley. My then master, Henry Herbert, detected my indebtedness to Bradley but he had never heard of Mrs. E. H. Brooke. When, later in my career, at the Old Vic, the London papers praised my interpretation, I tried to find the old lady, hoping she would come and see the fruits of the teatime talks, but she was dead.

Esmond Egerton-Hine, not a product of the Academy, whose performance of Gecko in *Trilby* was much admired, asked me to collaborate in a production of Browning's *A Blot in the 'Scutcheon* to be given in a hall one Sunday evening in the neighbourhood of Forest Hill, where he lived. I was to produce and play Earl Tresham, he to play Mertoun and business manager, and his wife Roberta, not a member of H.M.T. company, was to be the Gwendolen. I had met his charming wife, a vivacious, talkative girl, with a shock of prematurely white hair. I fancy she had talked Esmond into the idea. In one letter to her husband she intended inviting Mr. Tree to the performance. Esmond and myself certainly intended asking Joseph Harker to supply the scenery. The play was fresh in my mind from the Academy studies and the idea of producing was a flattering tribute.

We studied the play in dressing rooms, on train journeys, and scarecrows in the fields nodded approval of our ideas. Members of the company 'of our own kidney' agreed to fill the lesser roles and to appear as extras. Claude Rains accepted the stage management, he blew the gaff to Cecil King and King passed the news on to Mr. Tree. Esmond and myself stood before Mr. Tree in his dressing room. He was delighted with our enthusiasm but warned us that as soon as we were back in London rehearsals for *Antony and Cleopatra* would begin. We had better defer our preparations till after that first night 'and by the way, who is providing the money?'

The question stunned me for the financial side of our labour of love had never been discussed. But the business manager was on his toes, 'Well sir, when the people of the district see my wife billed as the leading lady I am sure they will support us'. 'Ah yes,' replied Mr. Tree, 'but who will pay for those bills?' Esmond again rose to the occasion, assuring Mr. Tree that his family would help us. Again we heard the inevitable prologue to a Tree reply, 'Ah yes, Ah yes—well, when the time comes if you need it, I will help you with a few pounds and if time permits me will attend your performance.' We trod on air, and Esmond wrote the good news to his Roberta. Alas! the bills were never posted and the only time I ever saw Roberta upon the stage was as *The Girl Who Took the Wrong Turning* at the Marlborough Theatre, Holloway.

This story has a sequel, for our youthful enthusiasm gave Mr. Tree an idea, and in the spring of 1907 in answer to an appeal from a working men's club situated off the Pentonville Road, he organised a Sunday performance of *Julius Caesar* to be given in the club premises and played by the small part, understudies, walking on and stage staff members of his company. He saw the performance from the Forum scene onwards and at the end received thanks from the club's chairman who assured Mr. Tree that 'Culture was marching on for the boys of the working classes in learning to speak the King's English and the daughters in playin' the piano'. The call boy Claude Rains played Cassius, the assistant stage manager Teddy Ruthven Casca, the stage staff provided the crowd and 1st and 2nd citizens, and I played Brutus, but of Brutus, more anon.

I was rather sorry when the tour was ended, I had learned so much, had enjoyed seeing England, loved the Sunday train journeys, with lunch provided by Mr. Tree, with hock from his own cellar, but back to London, where *His House in Order* had celebrated its 300th performance, and Lewis Waller playing Robin Hood on Shaftesbury Avenue—today you still see it on commercial television—and another of today's favourites, *Alice in Wonderland* was at the Vaudeville with Seymour Hicks as the Mad Hatter and Ellaline Terriss as Alice.

There was much to do among the old 'uns that Mr. George Alexander and Miss Irene Vanbrugh had allowed themselves to be photographed in their dressing rooms—making up—the mystery of the theatre was being invaded by the photographer. Yes, one felt that one belonged to a mystery—a race apart—alas, today, no longer. But the autumn at H.M.T. was full of activity. October 29th saw a revival of *Col. Newcome*, followed on 19 November by a revival of *Richard II*, and rehearsals for *Antony and Cleopatra* had begun. In

49

the *Richard II* revival I was promoted to the Bishop of Carlisle, and according to the press and my fellow players, I acquitted myself well. Viola Tree, who played the Queen, was most generous with her praise and told me that her father was very pleased with me. But I was deprived of my Bishopric on 8 December, the theatre being closed for the final and intensive rehearsals of *Antony and Cleopatra* which opened on 27 December 1906.

London had been destitute of *Antony and Cleopatra*'s for some years. In 1897 Louis Calvert had transferred his Manchester production with Janet Achurch as Cleo to the Olympic, and in 1900 Mr. and Mrs. F. R. Benson included the play in their Lyceum season, so London was agog with interest as to how Tree would handle his first attempt at the play and the part. Miss Collier's appearance as Cleopatra was eagerly awaited. One heard that the 'Hands off Shakespeare, Tree' factions were ready to howl down the anticipated spectacle that would destroy the play. I had read the play with care and during the early days of rehearsals talks with Fisher White, who was playing the Soothsayer, helped me to understand its wayward course. He had seen the Calvert production and hoped that Tree would make as good a job of it as Calvert had done, but he thought that Tree had miscast himself and Miss Collier.

I was no Shakespearean, just a small part actor, with the possibility of relegation to 'walk on' and understudy. My head was not buzzing with ideas as to how I would play Hamlet. I did play the 'moody Dane' during a tour with the Benson South Company, and all I remember is that I wore a black wig fashioned from a photograph of Matheson Lang in the role, and that I was not too bad in the nunnery scene.

At the age of 20 I dreamed that one day I would receive the plaudits of a packed house as the singing hero of a musical comedy—had I not during the 1903, as the solitary midday watchdog in the basement boxroom of a Luton warehouse, acted and sung the Toreador's song, complete with accepting the plaudits of my audience of boxes—no, the item was not from *Carmen*, but from the *Toreador** that I had seen at the old Gaiety during one of my crafty visits to London, ostensibly to see my mother—shame upon me, it was to get to a theatre.

Music still tugged at me, but while dreaming I had to tackle Ventidius with the lines of Canidius thrown in, a rather doggy part, not much barking but plenty of following, either Antony or Enobarbus, played by Lyn Harding.

In early December 1906, Arthur Bourchier produced *Macbeth* at the Garrick Theatre with himself and Miss Violet Vanburgh in the leads. We lapped up the notices. Many papers noted the simplicity of the mounting.

---

* A musical play, first produced 1901.

During a rehearsal of *Antony*, a loud explosion was heard from outside. The company stood still. 'Ah!' said Tree, 'Bourchier's head has burst.' The name of William Poel often cropped up during conversations, and Esmé Percy had told me of his attack on Irving's Shylock; it interested me to find that in 1904 the Rev. Stewart Headlam, president of the London Shakespeare League, with which Poel and Ben Greet were associated, had stated,

> To succeed, Shakespeare must be done in the Elizabethan manner, without scenery and, where possible, with the exits and entrances into the auditorium from the stage.
>
> We have to deliver Shakespeare from his two greatest enemies—the scene painter and scene builder on the one hand and the student or lecturer on the other, who thinks that Shakespeare can be understood in the armchair. By leaving Shakespeare to be dealt with in the Elizabethan way you are able to get the whole play acted in a reasonable time, and to get it acted with the actors properly balanced; the play is then indeed 'the thing'.

It was to be nine years before I met Ben Greet and Headlam, and my association with William Poel began in 1919. I knew little or nothing about the Elizabethan theatre but conversations, rummaging in books and press cuttings told me that William Archer has dealt harshly with Poel's Elizabethan performances and that my master's brother Max Beerbohm derided him.

Greet was not an out and out Elizabethan and had often quarrelled with Headlam on the matter, but George Bernard Shaw was a strong champion of the method. Tree was not impervious to the attacks upon his spectacular Shakespeare and defended his methods with a nervous and passionate sincerity. He termed his opponents as the adequats, and accused them of wishing to rob Shakespeare of the aids of modern science and art. Away with the adequats, he would cry—strange, in 1943 when Milton Rosmer took over the Stratford upon Avon festival from Iden Payne who had conducted a season of the plays in the Elizabethan manner, he cried *vide press*, 'Away with the Penthouse, give me back the scenery.'

The controversy is still being waged. The controversy of 1906 gave me a little food for a little thought, but what was good enough for Irving and Tree was good enough for me, but at back of my head I held a watching brief.

I wonder what the reaction of a modern audience would be to Tree's mounting of *Antony and Cleopatra*! I believe they would swallow it. It was magnificent. Rome was Rome and Egypt was Egypt. Tree departed a little from tradition by using, except for one scene, one scenic artist, Joseph Harker. Tricks there were—the play opened after a slow dimming of the house lights, accompanied by mysterious music, and the slow exposure on a front cloth of a magnificent picture of the Sphinx—it disappeared as slowly. At the end of the play the process was reversed. While Octavia was journeying from Athens to Rome, the public was regaled with a full stage tableau of Antony's return to Cleopatra—it occupied five minutes of time and gave Coleridge Taylor a grand opportunity. There were soldiers marching and counter-marching, swaying crowds, with a free fight or two, banners. Cleopatra stood upon her silver dais surrounded by her children, and I remember Tree's instructions to Miss Collier—'after I have embraced you, point to the children suggesting that you haven't been idle during my absence.'

Not necessary, but the management of the scene was the work of a genius and the public always expressed appreciation. Tree's version of the play opened with Shakespeare's Act I Scene IV followed by Antony and Cleopatra's first entrance, Philo's opening speech being given to Enobarbus and spoken after their first exit. Cleopatra's lovely moment, 'It is my birthday', was omitted as well as many other gems, but many gems were retained including the scene where the four soldiers hear 'Music i' the air', this under Tree's direction of the actors concerned and the lighting was a triumph of imaginative production. Tree had no time for the commentators and was rather ruthless with cuts and transition, but his version told the story.

One knew that the Shakespeare League would condemn Tree's handling of the great play, and it was a shock to me when working with William Poel in 1919 to find him not only a grand slasher of the text and an arch transitionist, but a re-writer of the verse. Little attention was given to the speaking of the verse as verse; one had to be human, and make the audience understand what you were saying and why you were saying it.

Fisher White kept an ear cocked on my rhythm, and in scenes with Enobarbus, Lyn Harding gave me useful tips. Tree gave him some useful hints, and upon Miss Collier he poured out his knowledge of the wiles of the Serpent of the Nile. His guidance of the Cleopatra scenes was an inspiring experience, he had an uncanny knowledge of women.

His mental approach to Antony was superb, but his voice lacked depth and there was no technique for sustained passages or declamation. He inhaled deeply but the stomach did more work than did the diaphragm. Fisher White pointed out these defects to me as a guidance for my future.

In her book, *Herbert and I*, Lady Tree refers to Antony as one of her illustrious husband's 'rare failures' in spite of the love, care and money expended upon it. During the run a revival of *The Red Lamp* was put into rehearsal together with an afterpiece, the one-act play *The Van Dyck*. In this I had the honour of being one of the three speaking parts, the others being

Mr. Tree and Mr. Weedon Grossmith. The play provided an hilarious 30 minutes and stood both Mr. Tree and H. B. Irving in good stead a year or two later, when the music halls, to bolster up the beginnings of their declining attraction, invited stage stars to appear in one-act plays. The *Van Dyck* would attract audiences of today.

Then came the most exciting news, His Majesty's Theatre company was to pay a visit to Berlin. This was I believe arranged at the express wish of His Majesty King Edward VII, who had a warm corner for Tree, and wanted the Germans to see what the leading actor manager of London could do without state aid.

The plays given were *Richard II, Twelfth Night, Trilby, The Merry Wives of Windsor, Hamlet* and *Antony and Cleopatra*, and played at New Royal Opera Theatre, really the Kroll Theatre that served as the Reichstag when the German Parliament was burned down. Additions to the company were Henry Neville, Nigel Playfair, Fred Lewis and Cicely Richards. Speculation was rife in London and Berlin as to the reception the Tree productions would receive. Mrs. Lyn Harding, who was German, obliged us with many titbits from the German press that suggested animosity from certain quarters and the two liaison officers, Mr. Max Hecht and Mr. J. T. Grein, close friends of Mr. Tree, reported from Berlin that the Germans were prepared to be very critical. The London platform was packed with well-wishers and the puff-puff from the engine was accompanied by resounding cheers as the train drew away.

At Hanover, the Mayor extended a civic welcome to Mr. Tree on the station platform and he replied in German. We arrived at Berlin on Monday evening 8 April 1907, and opened on Friday 12 April, with *Richard II*. I do not remember the address of the apartment where I slept and experienced my first continental breakfasts, but I do remember that the bed was very uncomfortable for I sank into the mattress and the top coverings were in a kind of bag that formed another mattress over you, very heavy and very hot.

As a young Englishman, following the popular trend, I distrusted the German Emperor and all his people and their bedding made me hate them, but on the Tuesday morning making my way along the Unter Den Linden, to rehearsal, a cavalcade approached, men stood still, raised their hats, clicked their heels, the German Emperor rode by, dressed in a light blue uniform, and I must say that he looked very fine. Little did I know at that moment that in a few days' time he was to pay me a signal honour.

Rehearsals were strenuous and went on far into the nights. No stone was left unturned to prevent a hitch in any department during the presentation. The German stage staff worked well under Cecil King and his interpreter, and His Majesty's Theatre's consulting electrical engineer, Mr. Digby, quickly mastered the Kroll Theatre's lighting technique. The master of Tree's music, Adolf Schmid, was at home. When not required at functions of welcome, Tree and his lovable liaison officers Hecht and Grein metaphorically took their coats off and with their fluent knowledge of the German language helped matters along.

A crew of German boys and girls were recruited for fairies, black, grey, green and white and sang 'Fie on sinful fantasy', in English. After their first rehearsal Tree's German extraction was apparent in his warm admiration of their prowess—they were good.

The Kaiser had placed at Tree's disposal members of a crack infantry regiment as soldiers for *Richard II*. They rehearsed well, but on the morning of 12 April, the opening day, they were not present, they had been marched away to Hanover. Rumour ran through the company, it is a German plot to ruin the performance. However, Hecht and Grein got busy, and a mistake was rectified with many Germanic apologies.

The morning of the 12th held another surprise. Fisher White was back as the Bishop of Carlisle and I was cast as Fitzwater and covered Fred Lewis as the Gardener. During the morning I was summoned to Mr. Tree who flabbergasted me by saying that I was to appear as the Gardener that night. No reason was given for the change. Viola Tree was the Queen and Tree supervised the rehearsal of the scene with meticulous care. During the afternoon Fisher White took me through the speeches. Before curtain rise Mr. Tree inspected my make-up, added a few deft touches and dispatched me to my dressing room with instructions to relax and not to be too anxious. I passed two hours of anxiety before making my entrance, for the German Emperor and all his Royal family, including Little Willie was to be in front.

The auditorium reeked with scent and after curtain rise the smell seeped across the footlights. A royal order was, no applause unless the Kaiser's hands dictated. I sat in my dressing room, I walked the passages and the moment came—I was acting before the German Emperor—came to the final line,

'In the remembrance of a weeping Queen'.

The curtain slowly fell—did I, or did I not hear—yes I did, I heard applause. The scene had pleased 'Kaiser Bill'.

Tree had watched the scene from the side and at the end of the performance showered congratulations upon me, his daughter was very complimentary too. J. T. Grein, a big noise in the London and continental theatres, was full of praise and Max Hecht, a power in Fleet Street, told me that I need never look back, adding that he would talk to me in London. From that day to this I have never discovered why Fred Lewis did not appear in the role he was billed for.

In *Twelfth Night* I played the Sea Captain, Dr. Oliver in *Trilby*, Marcellus in *Hamlet* and Ventidius in *Antony and Cleopatra*. My night off was the *Merry Wives* and with Harry Hewitt I scoured Berlin.

The German press was appreciative but guarded, the main wonder being that one man could do so much and so well without state aid. Of course the Emperor knew that King Edward VII had one eye cocked upon the nature of the German reception of his leading actor manager.

The gala night of the visit was *Antony and Cleopatra* and again the Imperial family honoured the English company, and again the theatre stank with scent. After the performance the company was invited to a buffet banquet to be served in the salon of the Opera House. But plots were afoot.

During the first half of the performance the German stage staff decided to go on strike, and when the time came for setting the tremendous tableau scene of Antony's return to Cleopatra, with the exception of a few of the electricians all had disappeared. Tree was in extremis, the Emperor was in front, a hold-up would be fatal, Grein and Hecht were arguing with the authorities of the theatre to command the men to return. But the situation did not defeat Cecil King, he appealed to the company and one and all we began to roll the heavy rostrum into position and handle the necessary furniture. King, and White, the carpenter, put flats into position and lowered the cloths.

But disaster—while the turmoil of the setting was at its height, and Tree was walking up and down, 'Oh! my Goding', someone, it was never discovered who, raised the curtain and the German Emperor was rewarded with the frenzied efforts of the English company obeying the English cry, 'the show must go on.' Applause greeted our efforts and somehow King managed to get the curtain down. The hold-up was not long, and we learned that the Emperor was highly delighted with the added piece of entertainment.

Hecht and Grein managed to get the staff to trickle back and all went fairly smoothly to the end. The reception and stand-up banquet was a slap-up affair, attended by the Diplomatic Corps, Berlin society and notables of the German theatre. My appeal to a waiter to serve me with two ice creams, wrapped in pineapple skins, standing on an out-of-reach shelf, was of no avail in spite of my pointing and reiterating *ein, zwei*. J. T. Grein, noticing that I was in trouble, offered to help. I explained that I could not make the waiter understand, so he took me to the waiter and introduced me to Max Reinhardt; I felt a fool, but he enjoyed the situation. But he did look like a waiter.

In 1927 I was in Berlin again and had to meet the great man at the Adlon Hotel. He was sitting at a very large table at one end of a very large room and as I walked towards him he rose, came towards me with outstretched arms and shouted 'Ah! Ice a Cream.'

Tree was a glutton for work, he disliked long runs and the members of his company found little time for mooning around. We left Berlin on 18 April and on the 22nd opened the 1907 Shakespeare Festival week at H.M.T., playing *The Tempest*, *The Winter's Tale*, *Hamlet*, *Twelfth Night*, *Julius Caesar* and *The Merry Wives of Windsor*. A routine bill for me.

A few performances of *The Red Lamp* and *The Van Dyck* followed, and on Monday 11 May *Julius Caesar* began a week's run, and thereby hangs a tale. On the Tuesday morning I received a telegram, not being on the telephone, requesting me to report at the theatre at 2 p.m. I found the entire company assembled and as I entered every eye was turned upon me. Mr. Tree put an arm around me and led me to a far corner of the stage and explained, rather falteringly, that the management had been caught napping, Mr. Basil Gill, the Brutus, had fallen sick, and there was no understudy ready; he, Mr. Tree, understood that I knew the part, would I be prepared to play it that night?

My head swam, here was a chance, could I take it, dare I attempt it. I stammered out that I knew most of it and that I could memorise the shaky bits. He took me by the hand and firmly walked me to the footlights, and said 'Ladies and gentlemen, Mr. Atkins will save us from disgrace.' The company applauded and the rehearsal began.

The shaky bits were noted and at the end of the rehearsal Mr. Tree took me up to the Dome, where I was to be left undisturbed to study. Tea would come to me and at 6.30 a light but nutritious meal, also would I like some-one to come up at my own time to hear me through. I elected 5.30 as the time and named a young lady member of the company. Tree blessed me and left me. It was an awful moment and but for the quiet but strong confidence I felt he had in me, I would have run away. However I got down to it, and walking and sitting I mentally worked through the part. Pacing the Baronial apartment, the Buchel frescoes of Mr. Tree in his famous roles seemed to shout encouragement. In the homely inner sanctum, the spirit of the man himself seemed to urge me on. Tea came in and at 5.30, the young lady. Half way through the hearing I decided to clean up a few shaky passages towards the end of the play and hope for the best. I was tired. A sleep, broken into by the arrival of a delicious meal, refreshed me and while eating Mr. Tree popped his head round the door, asking if I was all right, and bidding me not to rise, wished me to see him in his dressing room at a quarter to eight. After the meal I began to feel excited and walked to the top of the Haymarket and back to my dressing room. I waited upon Mr. Tree and after he had touched up my lips and eyes he implanted a kiss upon my forehead and thanked me for coming to his aid.

Thus at $20\frac{1}{2}$ years old I was to appear as Brutus in the leading theatre of the land with Mr. Tree as Mark Antony, Lyn Harding Cassius, Henry Neville Caesar, Fisher White Casca, Lionel Brough Citizen, Constance Collier Portia, Alice Crawford Calpurnia. I said a few comic things, including,

> Call Claudius and some other of my men;
> I'll have them sleep IN cushion ON my tent.

At curtain fall the company gave me an ovation. Mr. Tree embraced me, Viola who had been in front said I reminded her of Lewis Waller—praise indeed— and of course Fisher White beamed upon his pupil. Apart from Mr. Tree's evident appreciation of my effort the tribute that touched me most were the few words of encouragement spoken by the grand old veteran Henry Neville.

I played the role for the rest of the week, and received above my salary a cheque for £25. I felt on top of the world and blessed the name of Alexander Marsh whom I had seen play Brutus during my straw-hat days at Luton, and had caused me to plant the lines in my memory, and of course I had not been inattentive to the part during the few revivals I had played in at H.M.T.

Well I began to think, where do we go now? I didn't have to think, it was to a revival of *Trilby* after which *A Woman of No Importance* was to be revived, in which I was not cast. Disappointment was assuaged on hearing that after a few performances of the Wilde play a new front piece, *The Door upon the Latch*, a dramatisation by Kinsey Peile of Robert Louis Stevenson's story, *The Sire de Maledroit's Door* with Miss Collier, Mr. Harding, Mr. Gill and Mr. Atkins would be presented.

After criticising Lyn Harding rather harshly, the *Morning Post* reported 'The part of a monk, Dom Franciscus, was well played by Mr. Robert Atkins.' I think the play was put on to keep Miss Collier and Mr. Harding happy, it was not a good play.

Two or three nights a week, after shedding my monkish garb, I would beg Cecil King to allow me to creep into the O.P. Corner to watch Mr. Tree, Miss Ellis Jeffreys and Marion Terry in the main play. During the run my new-found champion Max Hecht, true to his words spoken in Berlin, contacted me and lunched me at the Café Royal, my first visit to the haunt of Bohemians. Being lunch-time the notorieties were absent. My host was in the rubber industry, very friendly with the magnates of Fleet Street and the leading men and women of the theatre. He had been a great friend of Sir Henry Irving and in 1899 joined Comyns Carr in forming the Lyceum company, which they hoped would relieve Sir Henry of his financial burdens. He wished me to work through my contract at His Majesty's and then he intended to guide me to further experience—alas, he died too soon. His son Henry I became friendly with and some time later I tickled the grand-daughter as she lay in her pram. Henry died too young, and for the time being I lost sight of the family. One summer morning, I think it was in 1941, I went to the Open Air Theatre, Regents Park, well before a rehearsal time and found a very beautiful, dark-haired girl sitting in the auditorium. 'Who are you?' I asked. 'My name is Maxine Hecht and I want a job. I have had no experience, but if you would give me a start I would be very grateful.' She was rather short in stature and a little on the plump side, but her face was very beautiful. She would certainly glitter up the extras, I thought, but the name, Hecht, rather dangerous under the war situation. 'Could you change your name?' I asked. 'Oh yes' came the quick reply, 'I intend to once I can get in, I live in South Audley and shall call myself Maxine Audley'. At this point my mind went back to Berlin in 1907—'You're not' I asked 'by any chance a relative of the late Max Hecht?' 'I am his grand-daughter' she proudly replied. 'Well,' I said, 'The last time I saw you I tickled you as you were lying in your pram'. And so Maxine Audley began her career.

The following appeal to Miss Audley's grandfather will delight Shavians. Tree in 1904 stoutly defended himself against the attacks made upon his *Tempest* production. The attacks were mainly against his treatment of the Shipwreck Shapes and Masque scenes. I never appeared in any of the *Tempest* revivals, but Elizabethan as I am now, my memory of the Island settings provokes me to say that nothing more simple or more beautiful has been seen upon the English stage.

Tree did not turn a deaf ear to the mutterings of his detractors—he has been styled 'a snapper-up of unconsidered trifles'—I quote from the 1915 edition of his book *Thoughts and Afterthoughts:*

> The art of stage presentation has progressed—and I think rightly pro-gressed—in the direction of a greater simplicity of treatment. In *Hamlet* I have found myself most happy in the purely suggestive surroundings of tapestries, and I have received assurances from many playgoers that they were more impressed by this mode of treating the play than by any other—it is the slow process of elimination of unessentials.

The slow process of elimination began during the 1907 run of the Wilde play, when three special matinees of *Hamlet* were given. I again played Marcellus and Viola Tree was the Ophelia. But the curtain setting did not eliminate one bar of the music composed by Sir George Henschel for the original 1892 production at the Haymarket.

Tree's inventive and lively brain was by no means hidebound to tradition with regard to stage settings, or business for the actors, but with the employment of music, tradition died hard. The Ghost was 'cello'd on and 'cello'd off, the King and Queen enjoyed the full orchestra, the Queen, describing the death of Ophelia, was supported by muted strings and clarinets playing broken snatches of the mad songs.

At the end of Tree's version, 'and flights of Angels sing thee to thy rest', an angelic host, of which I was a member, took up the line in a three-part musical setting, continuing until we were cued that Tree was dead.

At the second performance of this revival the Angelic Host went haywire and before we could recover ourselves Ophelia (Miss Tree) charged in among us, and pushing us right and left, shouted 'Oh! you devils, you devils, you've ruined my father's death.'

I recall the situation with levity, but at the time it was very serious and the Angels were on the carpet. Sir W. S. Gilbert's remark that Tree's Hamlet was funny without being vulgar had become a byword, and in seeking comparisons the inevitable answer was, 'Have you heard Forbes-Robertson's?' I had not, and the employment of the word 'heard', set me thinking. My beloved master's performance was sentimental, tender, satirical, and very picturesque; but how was he speaking Shakespeare? The answer came from my mentor Fisher White, who had a profound admiration for Tree in everything but Shakespeare, and so began a study of how Hamlet should be spoken. Another study was the character of Julius Caesar, which I was to play on the autumn tour, and as 'Fish', as we called him, would not be with us I took his ideas on vacation.

My London aunt and her jolly husband had moved to No. 1, Bartholomew Road, Kentish Town and graciously gave myself and my mother house room. I had seen very little of her and I began to learn how deeply both she and my father had longed to take up the theatre as a career. She was not unlike Ellen Terry in looks, and Irving had been her God. For Tree, I am sorry to say, she had no time at all as a Shakespearean actor. In literature her idol was Dickens and I caught the infection. She did like Tree as Fagin. There was a wide rift between her and the Luton sister and her husband, who had reared me, and my loyalty was at times stretched to a breaking point.

I do not think she liked my taking up the stage, it was I think a kind of jealousy that I might succeed where she had never had a chance. She loved me, but she loved the elder son more and the Luton treatment meted out to him was like poison in her inwards. I learned more from her of Irving's performances than from anyone in the theatre world. She was a truthful lady, so the following story must be true.

Her parents, Daniel and Maggie Evans, had a Welsh hatred for the theatre, it was Satan's Temple, but they were persuaded to go to the Lyceum once. At the fall of the curtain on Act I my grandmother nudged her husband,

pointer. He pointed us away from Haviland's movements back to the position of the 1875 production. I don't know if the knife gave him any inspiration, it certainly did not inspire Tree's company. A charming and gracious personality, but he left us in a muddle and all longed to see the blue eyes of Tree. The only part of Sir Squire's effort retained was the knife, for Tree used it. He didn't bother to see what had been arranged, but began all over again. Apart from the Shylock scenes, I don't think he was very conversant with the play and under him the first few rehearsals were a kind of what happens now, and a diligent study of the prompt book. But once he found his way his perception was seldom at fault. The scenes were massive and magnificent to look at, and all Jewry seemed to be in the cast, for my entrance on the Rialto to open the play broke into a host of Jews, magnificent specimens hired from the East End, haggling over the sale of their wares to Gentiles, and many a Yiddish expression floated into the auditorium. The articles for sale were theatrical props, but after a few nights they were found trying to sell genuine watches, rings and necklaces and if successful picking up the money at the end of the performance. This was stopped. During rehearsals their leader argued with Cecil King about their payment. King told him they were receiving the usual supers' rate. 'Ah,' said the leader 'You vant us for our faces, don't you?'. King admitted this. 'Vell,' replied the leader, 'You'll have to pay for them'. And the management did.

The Jews were used with much effect in the ghetto scene, where Shylock discovers that his daughter has decamped. An exterior scene with Shylock's house on one side and a synagogue on the other. From the centre the ghetto stretched to the Grand Canal and domes were seen across the water. The house was most realistic, the audience being able to see into the dining room and an upstairs bedroom, when Tree returned from his visit to Bassanio, he outdid Irving. He knocked upon the door, no reply, he tried the handle, the door was unlocked. He went inside, the audience saw him looking round the dining room with apprehension, they heard him run upstairs, saw him in the bedroom, heard him call Jessica and again Jessica as he came downstairs, back in the dining room he was frantically calling Jessica. His cries caught the attention of Jews in the synagogue who poured out and added their lamentations, including sounds of a shofa being sounded. As Tree in his agony turned to look Grand Canalwards a passing gondola was seen upon the skyline and with another agonising cry of Jessica, he turned to his door, to find a handy heap of ashes and prostrating himself, poured the ashes over his head accompanied by a song of lamentation from the sorrowing crowd.

This aid to Shakespeare was harshly criticised in many reviews, but Tree's answer came from his audiences, who seldom failed to applaud warmly what was a moving and magnificently produced effect enhanced by the fervour of the Jewish supers.

No Doge ever conducted a trial amidst more magnificent surroundings than did Doge Atkins, mounted high, canopied and limelighted. After the first rehearsal of the trial scene, Tree, thinking I might defeat the course of justice by showing too much sympathy for Antonio, asked me to play the part with the attitude of Pontius Pilate who during his retirement in Rome, in answer to the question of a young law student, did vaguely recall a famous trial in Jerusalem, but could not remember the name of the prisoner. Tree faulted with his casting for Portia and Nerissa and often during the trial scene groaned audibly at the inadequacy of the performances, but the Jessica of Miss Auriol Lee was a rare accomplishment. Tree's Shylock had moments of greatness, the scene with Leon M. Lion as Tubal was an exhibition of perfect racial understanding, and Haviland's phrasing was an object lesson for me.

This production of *The Merchant of Venice* drove me to Shakespeare and I began to wonder where I could get more experience. The answer came within a few weeks. From Dogedom I passed to Master Page to the Mistress Page of, I believe, Winifred Emery, and then came *Faust* by Stephen Phillips and J. Comyns Carr, in which I was cast for the Burgomaster, a short and stodgy part, but the production promised excitement and into my ken came three exacting personalities, Henry Ainley, Godfrey Tearle and Rosina Filippi. Marie Lohr, fresh from a triumph at the Haymarket, returned to His Majesty's to play a beautiful Margaret.

Tree was again challenging the memory of Irving, and on all sides the version he presented was adjudged superior to Sir Henry's. Many people preferred Tree's performance of Mephistopheles.

Apart from picking up crumbs of production, the run of *Faust* did not interest me very much. Of course I was watching fine acting, but was out of tune with my few lines and itching to get my teeth into something bigger. A respite came with Tree's inauguration of The Afternoon Theatre, the intention being the presentation of special non-commercial plays, produced by him but not of a necessity for him to appear in. I mentioned before that Tree disliked long runs and favoured the repertory system, but economics bound his hands and unfortunately the Afternoon Theatre did not prosper.

A start was made with William Archer's translation of Gerhart Hauptman's Dream Poem *Hannele* with a cast including:

Henry Ainley	Edmund Sass
J. Fisher White	Charles Quartermaine
Marie Linden	Norman Page

Clare Greet	Compton Coutts
Marie Lohr	Robert Atkins

I was cast for Seidel the Forester—another old man—but it was a good part and how grand I felt acting a scene with the golden voiced Henry Ainley. Little did I know then how he was to play me up some years hence. I made copious notes of the production which stood me in good stead when I revived the play at the Old Vic in December 1924.

After one rehearsal of *Hannele*, Tree, as was his wont, lovingly gossiping with his company, introduced the subject of further plays for the Afternoon Theatre and Marie Lohr begged him to play Richard III. With a sigh and a shaking of his head, he said, 'No, I saw Sir Henry Irving play it and I dare not'. Then King Lear was suggested and the reply was the same. Tree is depicted upon the walls of the famous Dome as Lear, but he never essayed the role.

Hannele was played on the afternoons of December 8th, 10th and 11th 1908, and the Afternoon Theatre died. *Faust* departed from the stage of His Majesty's on 15 December, and with it I departed too, to accept an offer from Henry Herbert, then leader of the F. R. Benson North company, to play Iago, Ford, Lucentio, Joseph Surface, the juvenile in *Richelieu* and with the extension of his repertoire such like parts of importance. Here was a chance indeed to get my teeth into something and test myself.

I knew it meant leaving a comfortable home and no longer proudly entering the stage door at His Majesty's as a member of Mr. Tree's company, but after a tussle with myself and the family, who thought I was mad, and a long conversation with Mr. Tree, who wished to retain me on a yearly contract, I decided to attempt the rougher experience. He wished me well and hoped that I would be with him again, finishing with, 'You may return here as a leading man'—a prophetic utterance in 1908—he later, as Sir Herbert, offered me work in *Macbeth* and *Othello* which I was not able to accept—my next appearance at His Majesty's Theatre was in 1936, when I returned to produce the play in which I spoke my first lines as a professional in a theatre, *Henry IV Part I*, with George Robey the Falstaff, and Lady Tree the Mistress Quickly.

CHAPTER FOUR

Bensonian?

I do not claim the title of Bensonian, the honour is for those who worked in the number one company, under Sir Frank himself. I do not think he saw me act, and the only time we were together on a stage was at Drury Lane when he appeared as Julius Caesar in an all-star matinee of the play, during which King George the Fifth knighted him, using a property sword.

I was one of the Forum mob. Apart from the excitement engendered by the royal action, I remember being surprised by the strength and muscularity of H. B. Irving, the Cassius, and that Arthur Bourchier, the Brutus, must have collected every scrap of tin, brass and iron he could lay his hands on for the battle scenes, for no Roman ever clanked as he did. The enemy must have heard his approach from miles away.

Henry Herbert was a Bensonian, beginning I believe in a humble capacity, but in 1908, when I joined him, his qualities as an actor and producer had made the Benson North company a profitable concern in the secondary touring dates allotted to it. He was ably aided by the business manager W. H. Savery. With Tree I had seen the cities and larger towns of the United Kingdom, with the Benson North I explored the cathedrals of Shrewsbury, Durham, Lincoln, Worcester and Hereford. The smoke of Stoke welcomed the company and Hanley, with its magnificent theatre, advertised for this visit, 'free list entirely suspended', and there was no bunkum about it. The railwaymen of Crewe had ears for Shakespeare and the digs were good.

Arriving late, one very wet Sunday evening at Perth, I remember knocking upon door after door in search of digs to be met with a blunt Scots, 'We no tak actors' and the slam of the door. I sampled the cake of Dundee and the horrible imposture of twice nightly Shakespeare at the Elephant and Castle, London.

It did not take me long to recognise in Henry Herbert a very fine actor and a more than helpful director. His productions were not copies of the Number One company's, but an individual approach, with settings, mostly of his own design, simple, realistic and artistic. At first I missed the glamour of Tree's settings but the importance of the actor became apparent. Herbert's detailed attention to Shakespeare's verse was illuminating and I learned from him its capacity for indicating the variation of character—and of sex, for he forced home upon his ladies the fact that their roles had been written for boys to speak.

I learned too, from a very clever member of the company, Arthur Fayne, son of Charles Fry, who had studied at the Paris Conservatoire, the pitch and stress of the Alexandrine. Herbert's trouble was an ungovernable temper, off and on stage. Once, when playing Friar Lawrence to this Romeo, he vented a rage upon innocent me by snatching the crucifix from my girdle and throwing it into the auditorium, much to the anger of the member of the audience whom it struck, and I was the innocent victim of his spleen as Macduff when during the fight scene Herbert Macbeth made a vicious unrehearsed thrust at my head and impaled my wig on the end of his sword, much to the amusement of the audience. Individual verbal attacks upon members of the company were commonplace.

Brilliant, at times, likeable but never loveable, Henry Herbert was a chronic example of the inferiority complex, engendered by his shortness of stature and lack of social background. A well modelled face, thin, but sensitive, a noble forehead, eyes that could split, or make a stone weep, and delicate and expressive hands. His delivery was clear and he passed on to his company his knowledge of the relative rapidity of rhythm.

I had read Molloy's *Life of Edmund Kean*, and likened Herbert to that wayward genius, perhaps more on stage than off, and with more consistency in performance. Certainly, Herbert's Lear was the best I have ever seen. He had a subtle and quiet sense of humour, but slapstick, which I heard him say was creeping into some of the number one company's performances, he eschewed.

During many squabbles aroused by his temper, oil was poured upon the troubled waters by his charming wife, Miss Gladys Vanderzee, the leading lady. During a performance of *The School for Scandal* she had the distinction, as Lady Teazle, of being found fast asleep when the screen was thrown down in the famous scene. I was playing Joseph Surface and Herbert's (the Sir Peter Teazle) quivering body alerted me for intervention, for I thought he would spring at her and strike her, but he stifled his ourtraged emotions. Poor lady, I think she'd had a bad day with him and had sought solace in a little liquid.

On joining the Benson North company each actor had to provide certain prerequisites for his wardrobe: one pair of black tights, one pair of brown, black velvet court shoes, and a pair of russets, a ballet shirt, scratch and juvenile wigs, and a pair of gauntlet gloves. Long beards were provided by the management, but whenever possible the mummer had to tease out his own crepe hair.

Depite much happiness, dear friendships made and the intoxication of public applause for one's efforts, I often wondered if I had done right in leaving London and would I ever get back. As an important member of the company I was receiving five pounds a week and had left a wife in London, for during the run of *Faust* I married the little lady* who came into the Dome to hear me through the lines of Brutus.

The wedding day brings back the memory of a sweet action by Tree. We were married one Saturday morning and observing the theatrical slogan that the show must go on, decided not to have a honeymoon; we couldn't afford it anyway, and as we entered the stage door for the matinee, Adolph Schmid and his orchestra, assembled on the stage, struck up the wedding march and Tree presented the bride with a bouquet of flowers, containing a cheque.

But away from the glamour of London how little did I know that I was laying the foundations for my eventual appearance at the Old Vic; for the experience with the Benson combination made me theatrically acquainted with fifteen of the Shakespeare plays, and I tackled such parts as Iago, Ford, Clarence, Lucentio, Prospero, Antonio, Brutus, Orsino, Gloucester, Jacques, plus Joseph Surface, a character that I found very difficult to put over. On the other hand my friend Cyril Sworder made a great success with Charles Surface and an early demise robbed the stage of a promising light comedian. An endearing friendship was that of brilliant little Andrew Leigh; his talent has been sadly neglected by West End managers.

In 1910, after much cogitation and serious talks with Henry Herbert and W. H. Savery, I was transferred to the Benson South fit up company, as leading man and producer, and owing to the lapses due to ill health of the business manager, often shouldered the business end of the outfit. Thus at an early age I found myself not only in command of artists, but also gaining an insight into the economics of running a touring company. In 1910, fit up touring was still an integral part of theatrical life, and on the whole very lucrative. The small town depended entirely upon the system for theatrical fare, and there was no competition apart from now and again a booth theatre operating in Farmer Giles' meadow. We struck one during a two-day visit to Falmouth and I saw a matinee performance of *Othello*. The Othello disobeyed the text by stabbing Desdemona many times and one heard the dagger piercing her corsage but unfortunately, on the final withdrawal of the weapon, a cabbage was affixed. A three-day visit to Truro found us up against tented mummers and they saw our matinee performance of *The School for Scandal* in which I played Sir Peter Teazle. In return

* Mary Sumner.

we saw their afternoon of a melodrama; the villain, as he disappeared down a well to hide from justice, interpolated a line from Sheridan: 'I go, I go, but I leave my character behind me Ha! Ha! Ha!'

At Truro we experienced the joy of dressing in the stables attached to the old Court House. During my two tours of the smalls I produced *The School for Scandal, The Rivals, She Stoops to Conquer, Hamlet, Macbeth, Othello* and *As You Like It*, playing Sir Peter, Old Absolute, Old Hardcastle, Hamlet, Macbeth, Iago and Jacques. We carried a good fit up, with a red and gold proscenium, red tabs, box sets and of course all the cloths were on the old fashioned tumblers.

The Shakespeare plays were all set with 12' cloths and wings. The management allowed my wife to join me to share the female leads and I remember with gratitude the work of Mr. and Mrs. Francis Roberts, she as the character woman and he as Macduff, Charles Surface, Othello etc. I enjoyed being a big fish in a very small pond and the production side of the experience began to interest me. I not only found that I could handle people, but found a joy in searching the texts for new interpretations and any sign of approval from the company flushed me with exhilaration.

It was grinding work, with one day, two day and three day stands, in halls comfortable and at times very uncomfortable. Cross-country train journeys in very uncomfortable carriages, diggings from good to indifferent, with the usual offices invariably at the bottom of the garden.

Anyway, I was the master man, the Beerbohm Tree of Penzance, Bideford, Weston-super-Mare, and how proud I was when my company played the three nights at my mother's birth place Llanelli, but pride had a fall on hearing that the Evanses of Llanelli did not approve of the theatre and I was further hurt when my great aunt told me that owing to family squabbles between the Evanses of Llanelli and London, the money from the tin mines would go to the Salvation Army.

However, the Llanelli press trumpeted my name up the Rhondda Valley to Mountain Ash. My head swelled a little when the North company notified me that some of the South profits had gone to the Number One company, then in financial difficulty. But an ill wind began to trouble the waters of my little pond, for my Lady Macbeth began to have ideas that I did not agree with. She was no Mrs. Siddons, and I had read enough to begin to wonder if the great Sarah did not disturb the balance of the play. Anyway I was the boss and Macbeth was the part, so I kicked her off the throne and replaced her by putting my wife in the role, intending to notify H.Q. after the occurrence. But the one disgruntled male member of the company did the notifying behind my back and down came Herbert. After hearing the evidence he agreed that artistically I was right, but had acted beyond my powers by deposing the Queen without seeking his consent. Had I done so he would have rid me of the lady altogether, but as the matter stood she would have to continue in the part for the rest of the tour.

I was stubborn, always have been, and said I would rather resign. So within a week, down came Baliol Holloway and his wife to take over, and we met for the first time. In a way I was not sorry about the incident as I might have drifted on too long in a state of smallish control. So, fortified with the added experience, I braced myself to face London again.

morning, with the added instruction that not only was I not to stay at Mr. Harvey's hotel, but also not to attempt to see him until Le Kurkamp arrived. I smarted under this high-handed treatment, no word of apology for detaining me overnight without warning, no mention of expenses, and to be told that I was not to lay my head under the same roof where Mr. Harvey pillowed. 'Oh, to hell with it!' I said to my friend Wright when he told me that a notice had been posted requesting the company not to recognise Mr. Harvey in the street. 'I can't afford it, but I'm going to book in at the Randolph', and I did and dead on time awaited Mr. Kurkamp on Sunday morning. He was late, and at 10.15 I requested the desk to ring Mr. Harvey's suite and I was lifted to the august presence. More charm was never poured upon a person. 'Sit down, my dear Atkins', effusive apologies for detaining me overnight— still no mention of expenses—'We won't wait for Kurkamp'. The diminutive man fascinated me, and the delicate face, quivering nostrils, waving right arm, and a voice that spanned two octaves wore me into an acceptance to play the Public Prosecutor in *The Only Way*, at the Lyceum Theatre, London at six pounds a week.

By the time Kurkamp arrived, furious that I had forestalled him, I was listening to stories of 'my great chief' as Harvey styled Irving and was left with no doubt that the mantle had fallen upon my new master, not upon Tree.

Kurkamp condescended to see me off the premises, drumming into my ears the greatness of Mr. Martin Harvey, and assuring me that my expenses would be met. On the way home I began to realise that I had been the victim of an amazing piece of acting; I had got a job, and in London, but the expenses were never refunded.

The Lyceum of 1911 was under the management of Walter and Frederick Melville, purveyors mainly of melodrama but to their credit the last upholders of the old-fashioned Christmas pantomime, transformation scenes included. The spirit of Irving had departed, possibly when his dressing room was done away with, although Martin Harvey did his best to bring it with him, even to the use of caustic remarks during rehearsals, but they were often the remarks of a petty man.

One morning, before rehearsal, a few of us chatting and smoking in the passageway leading to the stage door were called to attention by the entrance of the Chief; he allowed himself to be called Chief, as Irving was. The little figure, viewing us with disapproval, said 'Do you think it right to smoke in the Temple of Thespis?'

There was an aura around the man, but his conceit was unbearable. He had little sense of humour and when attempting to be jovial his speech became a series of dog barks. He was a picturesque actor and had moments of fineness and great beauty, but never really human. I don't believe he ever really felt an emotion, but he knew all the tricks. He loved and exploited his position of power, and many of his company feared him. No so Charles Glenny, the magnificent Defarge of the revival, who defied all the rules and regulations surrounding the great little man, as Mr. Harvey was called, and who was known to have slapped him on the back on meeting him in the street, and then roared with laughter, and the Chief admired him. There was the weak link, stand up to him and all pretence vanished.

The season opened on 11 May and ran through the summer. I did well on the Prosecutor and Mr. Harvey wished me to join the autumn tour, but I declined with thanks. I liked the members of the company but did not like the managerial atmosphere.

But I did enjoy the July interlude of four special matinee revivals of Maeterlinck's *Pelleas and Melisande*, with Mr. Harvey and Mrs. Patrick Camp- bell in their original parts. I played a servant and understudied Arthur Wontner as Golaud. An old friend from His Majesty's, James Hearn, was the Arkel and Alma Murray the Queen. The rehearsals were a delight; here was John Martin Harvey at his romantic and poetic best, and Mrs. Pat, who owned the play, in virtual command of rehearsals. Miss N. de Silva, Mrs. Harvey, was interested in the artistic side of the production, which annoyed Mrs. Pat who took no pains to hide the annoyance, and often after an interruption she would take it out of Pelleas by breaking off rehearsal and committing the unforgivable sin of smoking a cigarette and inviting Arthur Wontner to join her. Pelleas meekly waited. Another way of showing her contempt of an interruption was to pick up her little dog, and continue the rehearsal speaking her line to the dog's tummy as she tickled it. We marvelled at the patience of Pelleas.

We thought the end had come during the first dress rehearsal, when as Pelleas was fondling the hair of Melisande as she leaned from the turret window, the voice of interruption came from the stalls, and after a momen- tary pause Mrs. Pat shouted, 'Oh send that cow away'. Harvey's body quivered like a toledo blade, but a dove-like voice from the window coo'd, 'Remember, John, the play belongs to me'. The quivering body sagged, and the rehearsal proceeded.

Her beautiful performance made the powers that be forget and forgive the storm in a teacup that she created, and Master Harvey backed her up with a performance of equal beauty. The rehearsals were object lessons in the art of speaking as one listened to these two great artists bringing the lines of Maeterlinck to life, and the storms were grand entertainment.

Mr. Harvey parted with me with great affability and the usual hopes that I would be with him again. The hope came in 1930 when he offered me the part of Anderson in his Savoy production of Shaw's *The Devil's Disciple* but commitments prevented my accepting.

I saw much of him in his later life, spending many happy hours at his lovely home at Sheen. There in his study, wearing his velvet coat and cap, for he feared a draught, regaling me with whisky and cigars, he recalled the great days, of Irving, his god, and the Old Lyceum.

These memories are of a very gentle and loveable man, whose voice often came to me over the telephone, begging me to give work to his clever son Michael, and I often did so. Towards the end of the Lyceum season my wife whispered in my ear that I would become a father in the early days of 1912, so the need for further work was pressing and relief came from my old friend Fisher White, who was organising a music-hall tour of a one-act play by Scott Craven. I accepted, for the part—a Russian peasant, fighting nihilism—was a good one and I was to be given prominent billing and ten pounds a week, plus a promise from Fisher White, who was in the cast, to pick up the Shakespeare studies.

It was an experiment by the music-hall managers and all went well except at Sunderland. There we received a basketful of raspberries at every performance.

On one occasion performing seals showed their objection to our performance by barking through the thirty-minute duration of the play. What lovely people the music-hall artists were, so appreciative of one another's turns. They thought we were wonderful to hold a music-hall audience with a play containing neither singing, dancing or tumbling acts, among the top liners.

I met the lovely Marie Scott (delightful singer and dancer, and although I was an expectant father, I think I fell in love with her. I certainly saw more of the inside of her dressing room than I should have done), Charles Whittle, who was singing the rage song, something about 'The Ivy on the old Garden Wall', and the great comedian, Malcolm Scott, famous for his 'What does a billiard ball do when it stops rolling'—the answer being, looks round. A most erudite gentleman, his knowledge of world affairs, Shakespeare and the Restoration drama put me to shame.

It was at Hull, January 1912 that I received the news that I was the father of a boy. The first embarrassment of fatherhood occurred at the Hull GPO where despatching a telegram to a friend, which read, 'Today a boy', the middle-aged gentleman behind the counter, read the message aloud and more loudly added, 'and his name shall be Emanuel'. I picked up my change and rushed from the building. The weekend saw me in London and little did I think as I gazed at Ian Robert's brick-red face and mass of black hair, well down the nape of his neck, that in years to come he would be a big noise in the mechanical side of the world of entertainment, and a possible threat to the theatre as I knew it.

From the music-halls I went to the Glasgow repertory theatre, then under the guidance of Alfred Waring, to play Tybalt in a special revival of *Romeo and Juliet*. H. A. Saintsbury, the famous Sherlock Holmes, was Mercutio, Gordon Bailey Romeo, Lucy Wilson Juliet, and joy of joys, my dear old friend Mrs. E. H. Brooke, the nurse. It was a fine production and Lord Howard de Walden personally arranged the fights, with weapons supplied from his collection. George Whitelaw, the artist, was there on the Glasgow press and through him I made my first appearance in a paper in caricature.

Glasgow retained me for Galsworthy's *The Pigeon* and an interesting member of the cast, as guest artist, was John Clyde, the famous Rob Roy. Eliot Makeham and Percy Marmont were members of the stock company and they gave me many happy hours during my brief stay.

Before leaving Glasgow, I had received and accepted an offer from the Liverpool repertory company to play the Scots missionary Rankin in G. B. Shaw's *Captain Brassbound's Conversion*. The offer surprised me as the character was a middle-aged man. I learned later that someone concerned with the Liverpool company had seen me as the Bishop of Carlisle and had mixed me up with Fisher White, and on my arrival at Liverpool they were surprised, not to say nonplussed at my appearance. The facts that decided my acceptance were that Janet Achurch was playing Lady Cicely, her husband Charles Charrington was producing, and that to have appeared in a Shaw play might help me towards other modern work, and anyway a bash at character acting would do me no harm. Before leaving Glasgow, George Whitelaw took me through the part and gave me a good idea of the Scots pronunciation. I left Glasgow word perfect.

The first week of rehearsals were chaotic, Miss Achurch and her husband taking it in daily turn to be ill. Foul rumour had it that they shared dentures (a rehearsal in Miss Achurch's hotel bedroom proved the suggestion to be false), but she was not in good health. To William Archer and Bernard Shaw, Janet Achurch was the supreme Nora in Ibsen's play *A Doll's House*, and to me she was a supreme Lady Cicely. The quality and control of her voice was amazing and her movement bewitching. Her line to me, 'Don't you feel rather creepy, Mr. Rankin? I wonder what he'll be like', used to get a roar of laughter at every performance. You didn't act with her on the stage, you became the other person.

One night the message came round that Bernard Shaw was in the house, and after curtain fall I nervously awaited a verdict on my performance, but the author did not come round and to the end of the run no breath of his opinion came to the company. However, on my return to London I was overjoyed on receiving a letter from Miss Gertrude Kingston, saying that she was contemplating a revival of the play at the Little Theatre, and that Mr. Shaw insisted that if available I was to play Rankin. My hour had struck, I was on the top of the world, I had broken down the barrier that a Shakespeare actor could not tackle modern parts.

It was some years later that Mr. Shaw told me he preferred Shakespeare actors in his plays because they could open their mouths.

But alas, Miss Kingston's plans did not materialise and, armed with the letter that showed what Shaw thought of me, the search for work was on again. I think it was around this time that I met Maurice Elvey, who in conjunction with Miss Pam Robertson was running a Sunday society called 'The Adelphi Players' for the performance of unusual plays, and I dimly remember a stuffy back room in Maiden Lane where I played the Troll King in Ibsen's *Peer Gynt*. That was followed by a reading of the same author's *Olaf Liljikrans*, a play I think that has never been seen or heard of since.

Among the notables I had dropped a line to was Mr. Forbes-Robertson, and I received a very courteous reply wishing me to see him at his home in Bedford Square. I had seen him only in *Mice and Men* in which he played a dignified elderly gentleman. At the time of my interview he was 60 years old.

The door was opened by a butler, who showed me into the front room and then he came in. I looked at the most wonderful face I had ever seen, and his words of welcome came to my ears as the most beautiful voice I had ever heard. He wore morning dress and trailed a copy of *The Times*. Inviting me up to his study, he led the way, taking the stairs with difficulty, still trailing the newspaper. The first thing that caught my eye in the study was a large crucifix, the second a portrait of Sir Henry Irving. When sitting at his writing table, these objects faced him. Although over-awed by the face, voice and powerful dignity of the man, his simple address made me feel quite at home.

In my letter I had given him a complete list of my experience and this he went through very carefully, asking questions and making comments. Tree he loved both as a man and actor, and when he told me that Master Harvey was his first Osric, I noticed a gleam of devilment in his eyes. The reason for this I was to learn later. He was impressed with the work I had done, and although his company was almost complete he would do his best to fit me in, and would let me know. He did not ring for the butler to show me out but came to the front door himself and waved a goodbye from the doorstep.

Coincidences in life are strange. The post that brought the letter from Robertson expressing his deep regret at being unable to fit me in brought a request from Laurence Irving to see him. The night before I visited Irving I did not sleep a wink, not through excitement of meeting the actor I so admired, but because Ian Robert, who had some tummy trouble, yelled the whole night through. The doctor had told his mother to dip him into hot water, I think I suggested a total immersion, but with the morning came the sun and I was off to a Chelsea district to see Irving.

I found him a bit of a bear, grumpy, detached. I wondered if I would like him as a man, but he listened to my story, chirped up towards the end of the interview and smiled me away with the usual 'I will let you know.'

My theatrical sky was darkening and then the same post delivered a letter from Robertson and a postcard from Irving, both offering me a job. To me the letter was dignity, the postcard impudence. How dare the son of Sir Henry Irving write all the details of an engagement on a postcard for every Tom Dick and Harry postman to read? I was outraged, and plumped for the dignity of Robertson.

His farewell tour of England was to open on 23 September 1912 at Nottingham, to be followed in early 1913 by his farewell to London at Drury Lane and then to America for the first farewell tour. I now bless Laurence Irving and his postcard, for it was the Robertson engagement that led to the situation that proved to be the turning point in my career.

79

CHAPTER SIX

With Forbes-Robertson

THE Forbes-Robertson engagement completed my association with the giants of the Victorian and Edwardian Theatre. Tree was the full style actor manager; neither Harvey nor Robertson ever controlled a theatre. Tree was the greater man, Robertson the greater artist. Harvey never really conquered London, but in the provinces he shared the kingdom with Fred Terry and Matheson Lang.

The engagement with Robertson was a bit of a setback as far as parts were concerned, for he dragged me into the company at the last moment, certainly a compliment but I had to take pot luck and only in *Hamlet*, in which I played Marcellus and the Player King, did I measure up to my past experience. Bernard Shaw, who conducted the rehearsals of *Caesar and Cleopatra*, was pleased to see me and in my presence told Robertson how pleased he was with my performance of Rankin.

Rehearsing under Shaw was a new and invigorating experience, although my role was the few lines of the Centurion. I had to be content with Balthazar in *The Merchant of Venice*, Ludovico in *Othello* and with the few lines of Phil Raynor in *The Light that Failed*.

Understudy work was my lot in *The Passing of the Third Floor Back* and *Mice and Men*, and in *The Sacrament of Judas* I was a member of the firing squad. Compensation was listening to the voice, and watching the movements of the greatest classical actor of his time, the experience of seeing the length and breadth of the United States of America and Canada, and that during the western tours my wife was given the opportunity of showing what a very good actress she was.

The United Kingdom tour was indeed a royal progress, every mayor paying homage to the art of Forbes-Robertson. Civic banquets were frequent and his speeches both at receptions and at curtain call were the acme of brevity and dignity and never failing in expressing the hope that the future would see not only a National Theatre in London but a Civic Theatre in each large town.

No actor threw off the shackles of his career with more joy than Forbes-Robertson, for he disliked acting, but facing an audience he consecrated his artistic sensibilities to the job in hand.

When acting with Tree one had to be prepared for a flash of genius or intuitive change of mood or movement, but with Robertson there was no change of action, pace of delivery or intonation. The only interruption of the consistency of his performance came from a hacking cough but he most artfully spaced the affliction in the rhythm of his lines.

He was not a producer in the sense that Tree was, leaving the direction to his brother Ian Forbes-Robertson, but he knew what he wanted to do and where he wanted the artists playing a scene with him to be; positioning was a meticulous business with him. At one *Hamlet* rehearsal I remember well his difficulty in getting George Hayes, a splendid Osric, into the right kneeling position, and when satisfied said, 'That's the position, that's where Master Harvey was and I remember saying to myself, at last I can put my foot on the little b...'s head.'

I remembered the wicked gleam in his eyes when he spoke of Harvey during my first interview. He was temperate during rehearsals, showing more pain than anger at anything that displeased him, the one expletive being 'Christ', and that came from the bottom of his stomach.

The sound came to me twice as a novice at the 'royal and ancient' game on the Town Moor golf course at Newcastle. He played golf badly, and liked his company to play too—he organised a competition covering the tour, the winner receiving from him a set of clubs, and from Gertrude Elliott the bag in which to carry them. It had rained heavily overnight, and waiting to tee up I was nervously swinging my driver; swiped a puddle of water all over the dignified plus-foured figure of the great actor—a louder Christ was never heard; stumbling apologies; I tee'd up my ball, swiped, sliced the ball, which struck a tree and bounced back to my feet. The second 'Christ' was a sound of unbelief beyond belief—mortified, I picked up my ball and said I would begin at tee number two. I did not win the competition.

He was a tired man, and at times voice and memory suffered. At Manchester on making his first exit as Shylock his brother said to him, 'I suppose you know what you've done, Forbie, you haven't mentioned the pound of flesh.' 'Oh! dear', replied Robertson, 'well I don't think it matters, everybody knows the trial scene, but I mustn't do it again'.

I think he produced *The Merchant of Venice* to give his wife the opportunity of playing Portia, which she did with much charm, for the character of Shylock did not suit his personality, modelled though it was upon the performance of his first master, Samuel Phelps. Asking him whom he considered to be the greatest actor of his experience, he replied 'Samuel Phelps'. 'What, greater than Irving, Sir?' I said. 'Yes' he replied, 'because Phelps could speak'.

The answer to a poser, 'How many times do I use my full voice during a performance of *Hamlet*?' was, 'Seven'; the reason being that too much full voice might tire an audience, the seven times might bring them back for more.

The Company, chosen to fit a classic and modern repertoire, presented many styles of acting, from the perfection of Robertson, to me the most beautiful actor that did or ever will tread upon a stage, to the careful work of Gertrude Elliott, whose gifts as a comedienne were shown to perfection as Shaw's 'Cleopatra'; as Brittanus and Apollodorus, Ian Forbes-Robertson and George Hayes were brilliant. Shaw's verdict on Hayes's performance was 'The best ever Apollodorus'.

Frank Lacy, so good as Ruffio and the Jew in *The Passing of the Third Floor Back*, was with his very modern approach to Shakespeare a misfit as the King in *Hamlet* and received a rebuff from a Birmingham galleryite; for as Lacy spoke the King's line, 'Set me the stoups of wine upon the table', the voice from the 'gods' shouted, 'And give him a bleedin' fourpenny cigar'.

The irony was the playgoer's right pricing of the performance, for a Corona would have been out of the picture. A very amusing, and socially interesting member of the company was Adeline Bourne, an upholder of women's rights, and a distributor of the white feather. She kept Robertson primed with the affairs of state, for he loved to chatter politics and at times imagined himself in the Commons, but I think Canterbury would have fitted him better than the Exchequer. He was very patriotic, and after the bestowal of the knighthood, woe betide anyone who failed to address Miss Elliott as Lady Forbes.

No man wore the frock coat with such dignity as he, although the silk hat was always a little cocked to the right, a reminder perhaps of the rakish days. The London farewell season at Drury Lane was a story of packed houses and tremendous enthusiasm. J. H. Barnes, who when playing Bassanio with Irving and Ellen Terry, was known as 'handsome Jack', came in to play Polonius, so there was Hamlet aged 60, and Polonius, 63.

After the 'Lane' season the company were employed on a silent film of *Hamlet* under the direction of the then king of silent film makers, Cecil Hepworth. Studio work was done at Walton-on-Thames, the rampart scenes at Lulworth Cove, and the graveyard scene in the garden of Maxine Elliott's lovely home at Bushey. Robertson was not too keen on the idea and hoped to get out of it by stipulating that the play must be filmed as he played it; he was too tired to study a cut film version. Hepworth agreed.

It was a new experience for me, in fact I think for most of the company, and if a copy of the film is extant I wish the Film Society would exhibit a showing for I am sure that some of the shots would get bigger laughs than a

Charlie Chaplin effort gets. On the other hand a few shots show Forbes-Robertson as he was, many as an aged and tired man. Neither Miss Elliott nor Miss Bourne managed to walk gracefully, they just waddled all over the screen. For myself it was strange to see oneself mouthing the lines of the Player King with no sound. But the few pictures that show the facial beauty and princely bearing of Robertson would be worth a viewing.

[*Robert Atkins's account of his two North American tours with Forbes-Robertson leaves the reader with a very blurred outline of their itinerary. The first tour, opening in the autumn of 1913, began with a three month season in New York, followed by six months on the road. The second tour opened in Detroit, about September 1914; the company then travelled West to California and North to British Columbia. The leading lady on this tour was Laura Cowie, for whom Mary Sumner (Atkins's first wife) deputised when needed. The itinerary then turned East to Winnipeg. They returned to New York, where Columbia University conferred a Master of Arts degree on Forbes-Robertson on 2 June 1915.*]

Robertson was watchful for the comfort of his company and included my wife for the American tour. In the autumn of 1913 we sailed in the Franconia, leaving little Ian Robert with my aunt at Luton. The tour did not advance me professionally, it was the same old grind of parts, but to see the USA and Canada was a grand education, for during the two tours we visited every city and town of importance and I took every advantage to see the countryside.

It was a long while ago, but time cannot efface the memory of the many spots of beauty and grandeur. The smoke of Pittsburgh does not obliterate the beauty of wisteria cascaded Ithaca, nor the hectic rattle of Chicago, the quiet of Denver City and the solitudes of the adjacent foothills of the Rockies. The journey through the Rocky Mountains from Seattle to Canada was breathtaking.

The blue skies of California, Hollywood before the talkies came into being, the opium dens and the 'Barbary Coast' of San Francisco. Climbing Pike's Peak, on a mountain nag, and after the adventure not being able to sit down for two days and having to explain to Forbes-Robertson why I was hamstrung as the Player King that night.

During the Canadian winter people employed in the wildernesses of the country travelled distances up to 600 miles to the then modest townships of Regina, Calgary and Saskatoon to see the great actor. The length and breadth of the continent, his popularity was as great as was Irving's.

Unfortunately one was unable to see much of the American theatre in action, but in New York as an honorary member of the Lamb's Club I met many theatre personalities, including John Drew, David Warfield and David Belasco, the impresario who affected the wearing of a clergyman's collar. The actor who impressed me most was Leo Dietrichstein; the actresses, Maude Adam, Laurette Tayor, the beautiful Elsie Ferguson, and of course Ethel Barrymore. Although the New York critics viewed the visit with a Hail and Farewell spirit, there was more vinegar in their inkpots than in the inkwells of London.

One inspired gentleman wrote, 'If you wish to experience the taste of drinking pink tea, go and see Forbes-Robertson play Othello'. Of my performance of the Player King, the same gentleman penned, 'There is nothing in Shakespeare's text to suggest that the actor of the part should not be an actor of the first rank'. I did not let the editor into the secret that I had been instructed to play the role as a second-rate mummer.

The summer of 1914 saw me back in London and contracted for the second American tour opening in the autumn, but the war broke out and with now Sir Johnston's permission I presented myself at the recruiting office at Great Scotland Yard and to my great surprise was rejected and given no reason why. My own doctor was in no doubt, there was the danger of middle ear trouble in my right ear and he advised me to have constant medical attention.

Under the circumstances Sir Johnston persuaded me to return with him, hoping, as so many people did, that the struggle would be a short one; anyway, he said, if the war is still on when we get back you can try again. We sailed on the old SS Grampian and she literally rolled every inch of the way to Boston.

During the tour I paid many visits to doctors for ear attention and one gave me the cheerful news that my left ear was in a poor condition too. In Canada I tried to join the Canadian forces but was again turned down.

This to me unhappy tour had a bright side. Lady Forbes was left in England to have a baby and Laura Cowie was the leading lady. Somewhere on the Pacific coast she fell ill and had to be left behind, and my wife, Mary Sumner, took over the leads in *Hamlet*, *The Light that Failed*, *Mice and Men* and *The Passing of the Third Floor Back*. Sir Johnston was delighted with her, so were we all. An added triumph to her really beautiful performance was that she was not the understudy, but had taken the trouble to learn the roles and watch during performances. It was Ian Forbes-Robertson's knowledge of this fact and his belief in her that persuaded Sir Johnston to give her a chance.

I think it was in the theatre foyer at Montreal that Sir Johnston unveiled a memorial plaque to the memory of Laurence Irving and we were rather horrified to hear the Canadian dignitary in charge request Mr. Robertson to unveil the memorial to Sir Irving. A whispered direction quickly brought from the gentleman: 'Oh! I do beg your pardon, Sir Raaaabson'. The American people showed little interest in the war, even to not caring which side won. The *Lusitania* had not been sunk and the only hostility to the English Company was in San Francisco, fanned by the German colony.

Israel Zangwill was stumping the country on behalf of the British cause and getting himself into hot water for his attack on what he termed the American inactivity. His play *We Moderns* had been produced in Washington and he received the blessing of President Wilson, but wherever the play went, the drum of hostility against Zangwill had sounded and the play was taken off the road.

Newspaper headlines announcing a British setback were far larger than the news of the Germans in trouble, but one headline in a Cleveland paper topped the lot for size, and it was with reference to a past domestic war. Mrs. Patrick Campbell was playing in the opposite theatre and staying at the same hotel as Sir Johnston, and the headline ran:

Mrs. Pat Campbell and Sir Robertson staying at same hotel—will they?

I have not visited America since 1915 and I would like to see and hear it again and again enjoy some of the food. I believe the noise of the elevated railways in New York and Chicago is less clattering but I hope the waiters in Childs' restaurants are still shouting, 'Eggs on both sides', and that the consumption of baked apples and waffles with maple syrup is still accompanied by the sound of crockery being hurled down the washing-up ramps.

The noise of Harlem and the downtown singing, chatter and shouting of the negroes in Baltimore, the noise of an American baseball or football crowd, can never be forgotten and if, when on the road, one's hotel was near the railroad, the clang of the locomotive bells was often a nightly disturbance.

One missed the roast beef of Old England and green vegetables are often a pap, and if you wanted a cup of tea, well you had to make it yourself, but when the purse allowed, a planked shad or steak was something the old country could not serve up. The luscious three-tier club sandwich was introduced to me at Yale by George Pierce Baker, the founder of the famous 47 Theatre Shop. I met him again at Harvard where he founded his well-known University Theatre workshop, and although not a professional he was the most interesting and inspiring man of the theatre I met in America.

He was regarded as largely responsible for the development of American playwriting and contended that every budding dramatist should go through the production mill so that he would realise the technical problems he was posing. His students of dramatic technique were required to build, paint and handle scenery, as well as to act and direct. Strindberg acknowledged the inspiration he received from Baker.

It was in April 1916, at the Harvard University's Sheldon Lecture Theatre, fashioned I believe for the purpose by George Pierce Baker to a copy of the Elizabethan Fortune Theatre, that Sir Johnston Forbes-Robertson made his final appearance upon a stage, as Hamlet. I was not with him at the time, being back in England, preparing to say 'Who's there—stand and unfold yourself' in the costume of an English soldier. Of the thirty five Hamlets I have seen, played with or directed, Sir Johnston, even at the age of sixty, was the most perfect. Nature helped him with a voice, face and bearing that made him a Prince. He was the master of fluent and impetuous diction and did not cast about for subtleties of meaning which Shakespeare did not intend. He sought his effects not only in the perfect speaking of lines, but in the use of words.

Standing on the stage with him as Marcellus, at every performance, the agonising beauty of his use of the three words to the Ghost, 'Oh! answer me', made my stomach turn over. The vowel sounds of the English language were music to him. Then he was a Celt. He found more humour than any Hamlet I have listened to; his speech to the players was in the vein of the serio-comic. I seldom missed listening to his delivery of the 'Oh, what a rogue and peasant slave am I' speech; it was a drama in itself.

I have been moved during performance by many Hamlets, but the voices have faded. Sir Johnston's speaking of Hamlet will ring in my ears till I shuffle off this mortal coil.

THE PIERROT FAMILY AT HOME

1: As Shylock (above) and as M. Pierrot in *L'Enfant Prodigue* 1906.

2: As Ventidius, with Lyn Harding as Enobarbus 1906.

3: *above*, With Lilian Baylis and stage staff. *below*, With Hubert Hine (stage manager). Old Vic 1921.

4: As Cardinal Wolsey 1925.

5: With Lilian Baylis. First Folio completed. Old Vic 1920–25.

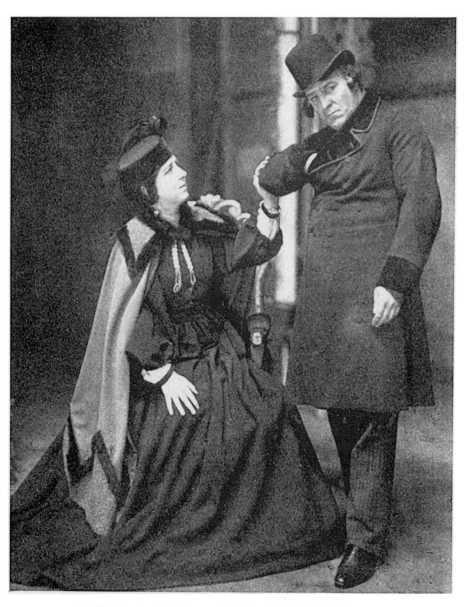

6: With Margaret Scudamore in *Trelawny of the 'Wells'* 1926.

7: As Bottom 1933.

8: As Caliban 1933.

CHAPTER SEVEN

The Old Vic 1915–1916

BACK in London at the conclusion of the American 1915 Spring tour, I hurried to the recruiting office at Great Scotland Yard, to be told that I would be classed B.1 owing to the danger of middle ear trouble in my right ear, and would receive the call up in due course under the Derby scheme.

I was not particularly anxious to stick a bayonet into anyone, but I did want to 'do my bit' as an A.1 man so arranged with my own doctor to undergo a course of treatment, hoping that when the call up came I would be fit for the front line.

In answer to the question, which day would I consider to have been the most important in my life, I would say the day in the spring of 1915 when I ran into my old friend of His Majesty's Theatre days, Fisher White. He suggested that I filled in the time of waiting by helping Miss Lilian Baylis at the Old Vic and gave me a letter of introduction. I was interviewed by Mr. Philip Ben Greet (later Sir Philip), the then director of the plays at the Old Vic, who fortunately remembered some of my work with Tree, and offered me three pounds a week to stage-manage and play parts. After hearing some of the plays that would be produced I said 'Yes' on condition that I played Iago, Cassius and Richard III. My conditions took him aback so he took me to see Miss Baylis.

She was sitting at a large roll top desk that occupied at least a quarter of the not overspacious office. A very Victorian sofa, a table, two or three chairs and above the fireplace a large corner cupboard completed the clutter. Below the fireplace, on the floor, was a gas ring upon which rested a frying pan in which pork chops and potatoes were sizzling. During the interview a Miss Muriel Ellis popped in and out and tenderly turned the contents of the pan. Both Ben Greet and Miss Baylis were generously proportioned, and between their figures, the furniture, the flitting Ellis and the smell of the cooking I felt a bit hemmed in.

The downward twist of her mouth disconcerted me, and she seemed rather common, but the eyes were very kindly. She required hard work and a devotion to her cause, her Theatre. The wages were starvation but the theatre café, Pierce and Plenty, would give me a good steak for fourpence. Exclaiming that she liked my face, she waved aside Greet's objections to my demand for certain parts, saying 'If he doesn't rehearse well, kick him out', and the bargain was clinched, and (her very words) I was to 'muck in' at once.

Fisher White had warned me of Miss Baylis's religious activities, but at this first meeting God was not mentioned. So until I collected the King's 'shilling' I laboured at the old dirty, dusty 'Old Vic', and it became a labour of love and purpose; for with all her comicalities I began to realise that Miss Baylis had planted a creative weed. But the soil was rough, for the stage was knotty, and the flats supported by the old fashioned grooves. Front curtain and scenic cloths rose and fell on heavy tumblers and often fell with a heavy bump during performance. The footlights were incandescent, and number one batten, naked flames caged with wire. The six brass handles governing the supply of gas were worn out, and often during a lighting change both footlights and batten would pop out.

Then Old Bob, the stage door keeper and jack of all trades, would appear with a lighted taper to re-illumine the scene. He was greeted with laughter and disappeared to applause. The auditorium was dotted with framed panes of looking glass taken from the one-time glass act drop that pulled down the proscenium by its inordinate weight, and before and behind lavatory and waiting facilities were primitive.

The environs presented by day and night a seething mass of purveying and buying humanity, the coster and Jewish voices prevailing. They were often entertaining but at times terrifying, for many a murderous quarrel took place when the naphtha lamps were flaring above the market stalls of the New Cut and Lower Marsh.

The small box office and foyer entrance to the theatre occupied the left hand corner of the frontage, the other corner being adorned by Messrs. Pierce and Plenty's Café where upon marble topped tables and with one's feet in sawdust the aforesaid juicy fourpenny steak could be enjoyed, or a pint of tea, in a china mug, with a slab of bread and butter for twopence. Other delicacies offered were a penny basin of 'peas duff' or a slab of 'Happy Spotted'—the local name for plum or currant pudding.

Many a happy rehearsal break did I spend in the Café, sipping a pint mug of tea in the company of Miss Sybil Thorndike, the leading lady, and other members of the company including William Stack and Florence Saunders; and how proud we were in the interest shown in us by the nobility and gentry of the New Cut, as Gasfitter Gerridge in *Caste* termed them, as they sipped their tea, for no strong drink was allowed within the four walls of 'Queen Victoria's Own Theatre' as the locals called it. Many of them were patrons, for the price of admission, fourpence in the gallery to five shillings in the stalls, was well within their pockets.

An amusing memory is the business all around the Old Vic in 'Lord Mayors', the slang term for odd pairs of boots and shoes, matched into pairs as far as possible and laid out in rows upon the kerb.

Facing the Waterloo Road side of the theatre was the shop of Mr. Hurry, the undertaker, his neighbour being a gin palace, a frightening spectacle on a Saturday night, and no lady member of the cast was allowed to leave the theatre without a male escort. The area was dotted with hairdressing salons, and from the outside many suggested that the head wielder of the razor might be a Sweeney Todd. From the doorstep of the 1915 Old Vic the scene contained Jewish tallymen displaying hand-me-downs, purveyors of jellied eels and whelks, and a steamy cook-shop where one could buy half a baked 'Jimmy' (a sheep's head) for a few pence.

I often wandered through the Cut and Lower Marsh, where of course I became known, and from this phantasmagoria, in my mind's eye, could cast many a Mine Host, a Nym or Pistol or Bardolph, a Jack Cade, Mine Hostess and of course a Doll Tearsheet.

A rough jumble of humanity with many a kindly heart among them, and many a patron of what we were striving to create within the walls of the theatre in their midst. It was from this class of people that Miss Baylis wished approval and from this class she hoped the pennies would come to bring her work to fruition, for to her, a penny from the gutter meant more than a cheque for £100 from a prince. Well do I remember the year 1923, when we were faced with 'rebuild or close.' The pennies did not roll in, and with the £30,000 worth of salvation coming from one man, although delighted that her theatre was saved, the blow to her 'penny' hopes was severe. One had to understand this strange lady's penny attitude to life really to understand her. But back to the hard seated pit and the glass panelled structure between it and the back wall of the auditorium of 1915.

It was soon clear to me that the opera was the 'be all' of Miss Baylis's outlook, and very clear to me that she knew very little about Shakespeare beyond the titles. But she had a good ear for the spoken word, and was much attached to a 'form' as she termed a male torso that appealed to her. It at times suggested another meaning, as when telling an actor, wearing tights that exposed the stomach, to hide his form a little.

The opera, presented on Thursday and Saturday nights, invariably played to packed houses, the management playing the safe game of dishing up the old favourites: *Carmen, Faust, Martha, The Lily of Killarney* and of course *Cav* and *Pag*. Wagner was creeping in with *Tannhäuser* and *Lohengrin* and Mozart's *Don Giovanni* received a warm welcome, but an attempt to present The *Elijah* in dramatic form left the musical patrons of the then Old Vic stone cold; they preferred *The Last Rose of Summer*.

from asthma and when on parade was followed by his batman carrying a throat spray—when the batman was ordered to give a squirt it reminded one of a mother bird feeding its young. When mounted, the CO would snatch the spray and perform the operation himself.

He was fond of parading men in the heat of the day and if a man succumbed he would bark out the order, 'Carry the b... away'. A grain of sand found in the metal top of a pith helmet was a crime, although during the inspection the wind was raising the sand. But the British Tommy always gets his own back, as witness the scene on the railway siding when he was seeing a trainload of men away up the line. On the point of departure every window was full of as many heads as could be pushed through and the imprecations hurled at the CO were terrible to hear. But he stood to attention and God Blessed them, and the more he God Blessed, the more terrible were the words that floated into the desert air.

At that moment I certainly admired that most unpopular soldier as he stood unperturbed at the abuse hurled at him, for I am sure he was sincere in the belief that his harsh methods were the only way to assume that everyone under his command did his duty to King and Country.

The RSM was a chip off the Guards block, but with a grim sense of humour, my instructions being, when left in charge of a squad for form fouring and quick marching, to 'Give 'em bloody hell'.

Off duty tramway jaunts to Cairo eased the tension of many hours. The 'Moussky' had not begun to lose the eastern authenticity, although here and there one could spot a piece of brass from Birmingham. The Mosques were havens of rest, and in the El Azrah the drone of the students of the Koran made me begin to realise that the Christian faith was not the faith of all peoples.

Bred a Baptist, baptised into no faith, in the army C of E, I had given little or no thought to the religion of the world. This stirring of my mind in the El Azrah had a pleasant sequel some months later at Kantara.

A man's best friend is his rifle, was the slogan of my instructor in musketry. My best friend gained me full marks as a marksman, but I didn't care much for sticking a bayonet into a stuffed sack; anyway I wasn't very good at it, and flinging Mills bombs always scared me stiff. How happy I was after practice to find that I had eight fingers and two thumbs. Eventually, self and best friend arrived at Lydda, the railhead, ready for active service.

I poked my nose and gun into Gaza, Hebron, Nablus and was on guard duty in Tel Aviv when the Balfour Declaration was read; my chief memory of this historic occasion is of the hundreds of Jewish girls wearing white frocks and blue sashes. A pleasant break in active service was when I was sent back to Kantara in charge of 30 'details' and told on arrival that nobody knew who we were or why we were. The orders were to lie low until the great discovery was established. This took three weeks, the upshot being that I was packed back up the line with my 30 men still undiscovered.

During those three lovely lazy weeks I met a Padre who had seen me at Drury Lane and to him I mentioned my thoughts during my visit to the El Azrah; he loaned me books on theology. Each evening I swam in the Suez Canal and floating, noted the changing colours of the wonderful sunsets. The effects were noted on paper and came in very handy for future theatrical purposes.

Back up the line for the clean up, and during a rehearsal for advancing to the attack in platoon formation an amusing incident occurred. In charge of a platoon, I gave the order to advance, when from the rear came 'Hi! hi! hi!'. I dropped my men and turned, and saw the fellow in charge of the platoon behind running towards me. I ran to him thinking something had gone wrong, and to my astonishment heard, 'Didn't I see you play the Bishop of Carlisle at His Majesty's Theatre?' I cursed him up hill and down dale, telling him to get on with his job. Meeting afterwards he said he recognised my voice when giving the commands. The story of the hold up had to be told and the poor chap was severely reprimanded, but the incident caused amusement.

North of Jaffa, waiting to be picked up by an ambulance, I dreamed the soldier's dream of a bed with white sheets and a female nurse to minister unto one, but alas, I was trundled back to Tel Aviv, my bed was my stretcher, and I had forgotten that no female nurse was allowed beyond the railhead: the nurse was an Indian orderly who tucked me up in army blankets. The hospital was a school building presented to the town by the Kaiser.

Doctors were scarce, one popping in every three or four days, and we learned to tend each others' wounds. Fortunately all were fairly light cases. During convalescence the sea breeze was a pleasant change from the torrid heat of the interior, and meandering through the streets of Jaffa, reminding me of my Sunday school days and the story of the good works of Dorcas, and in the quietude of the dirty old streets, away from the noise of war, one realised that we were in the land of the holy story.

On rejoining the unit our job was to bring in the prisoners. It was the saddest sight of my war experience, for the Turkish army was in a deplorable state of sickness and filth. Many officers had their wives and children with them.

Bringing in one batch, a Turkish Sergeant Major would walk with me, he was 6' 6", a massive figure, and a ferocious black beard. He laughed and laughed and laughed, and shouted something like 'Lo, Lo, Lo, bom, bom,

bom' waving his arm joyfully. I expected at any moment to feel his fists cracking my skull. When I got him behind the wire I asked an interpreter what he was trying to tell me. His explanation was that London had been bombed to the ground, his authority being the Austrian troops serving with Turks.

I cannot remember exactly where it was, but during July 1917 I was summoned to the CO who told me that he had received the news of a death of a friend of mine, Sir Herbert Tree. I felt very proud of the term friend, and thought it a grand gesture of the CO.

The desert stretches and the hills of Palestine, with the maddening sun and the more maddening moon and the wind and rain of the winter season, are not an endearing memory, but like many soldiers I look back with pleasure to many happy times during the campaign, the happiest memory perhaps the friendship of many men. After the armistice in the Eastern Theatre of War, the Battalion was ordered back to Alexandria, via Kantara, where we were halted for a month to undergo, to our disgust, heavy peacetime training, including forming fours all over again. This was I think to keep the officers busy and to allay a serious feeling of unrest in the British army from Damascus to Alexandria owing to poor food and the authority's deaf ear to the men's clamour of 'We want to go home'.

In the early days of 1919 the unrest began to assume an ugly nature and I witnessed the amazing sight of mass meetings of soldiers in the Mohamet Ali Square in Alexandria being addressed by uniformed 'soapbox' orators.

During the mass meetings, hundreds of 'Gypos', fearing the British army was planning to attack them, climbed to the rooftops, out of harm's way. Results of the haranguing were that the rank and file refused to salute officers, and mounted guard under protest. The authorities dealt very wisely with the situation and the men began to trickle home.

Waiting for my release I was much occupied, by command of the CO, with Mrs. McMinn and her entertainments, producing *The Marriage of Kitty* and *The Second Mrs. Tanqueray* at the Alhambra Theatre in aid of St. Dunstan's.

Then came the day when I packed up, and via Port Said, sailed for home, not demobbed, but on leave, being told with a wink to pull all the strings I could to get out. I arrived home in May 1919, and the strings were pulled by Peter Davey, manager of the Theatre Royal, Portsmouth who gave me two weeks' engagement to play in *The Two Little Vagabonds* and *The Sailor's Wedding*.

Armed with employment I was directed to the Crystal Palace for demobilisation, and came face to face with my first CO of Portsmouth, who exclaimed 'Good heavens, it's Ben Greet's Macbeth'. Well Macbeth left Sydenham Hill, a free man. On the whole I had a good war, with much discomfort, certain dangers, but with memories of deeply interesting and happy days, and losing a decoration in the toss-up.

One evening, with the knowledge that tricky work lay before the troops at zero hour, I had begun to wonder what I could do if I were maimed and unable to act, and the idea of production came to my mind. By candle light I wrote a rather jocular letter to Miss Baylis expressing my ideas on the way Shakespeare should be played. I jokingly transformed the construction of the stage and lighting equipment, appending a list of plays for my first season. In 1920 the programme was presented at the Old Vic under my direction, plus the transformation.

CHAPTER NINE

The Old Vic 1920–1925

[*In the early summer of 1919 Atkins appeared as Quin in Ben Greet's tour of* Masks and Faces, *opening at* 'a long-forgotten theatre in Muswell Hill' *and finishing at the theatre in the Crystal Palace complex, Sydenham, South London.*

This tour was followed by an engagement to understudy Norman McKinnel in Robert Hitchens's The Voice of the Minaret *at the Globe in August 1919. It was during this stint that William Poel approached him, as recounted in the following chapter.*

There may well be a connection between Atkins's work for Poel and Lilian Baylis's decision to implement her promise of four years earlier and invite him back to the Old Vic, this time as director of productions.]

In the early stages of my five years at the Old Vic, I was on the theatrical map, as far as Shakespearean productions were concerned. I will quote from an article written in 1921 by Herbert Farjeon, the well known dramatic critic and Shakespearean authority, entitled 'Some notes on the Old Vic and its unsurpassed Shakespearean production'.

> One evening this autumn, 1921, at a symposium of dramatic critics, the writer of the present article was asked to name the most important theatre in London. Unhesitatingly he answered 'the Old Vic'. And the assembled company endorsed his verdict. The Old Vic may not be Shakespeare's spiritual home: his spiritual home is the Old Globe on the Bankside where the environment was peculiarly adapted to the requirements of his plays, but Mr. Robert Atkins has brought to bear on them a sympathy, an insight, and a fundamental appreciation of the essentially practical beauty of the poet's creations such as no other manager of the century has displayed. The productions at the Old Vic are swift, simple and to the point; and if Mr. Atkins has yet far to travel before he reaches the only destination worth making for, he is well on the right road. Last season when Mr. Atkins took over the practical management of the plays the theatre emerged for the first time out of the rut of the commonplace.'

Mr. Farjeon's reference to the 'right road' pleased me, for it meant that I was profiting from my experience with William Poel. Praise and helpful criticism came too from such luminaries of the critical world as G. E. Morrison of the then *Morning Post*, E. A. Baughan, *Daily News*, H. M. Walbrook, *Daily Telegraph*. A. B. Walkley of *The Times* never appeared, but the dour William Archer sometimes invited the readers of *The Star* to pay us a visit.

The attention pleased Miss Baylis, for Fleet Street had been spare of its attendance in the past. A little unfair perhaps, because my immediate predecessors, Russell Thorndike and Warburton, who shared productions and male leads, were very gifted performers and had with them the very beautiful and gifted Florence Saunders. Katherine Willard, an American actress, and Orlando Barnet were talented artists and with Andrew Leigh popping in and out, the nucleus of the company was worthy of attention. The pawky little Scot, Hay Petrie, a beginner, was already showing signs of becoming, as he did under my regime, a genius for Shakespearean clownship. Wilfrid Walter too, then the scenic artist, signed on with me and turning his mind to acting gave in due course some notable performances.

Thorndike returned in 1922 to give the performance of his life in *Peer Gynt*. This production was the turning point in the fortunes of the Old Vic, for the West End flocked over the Waterloo Bridge to see the first production of Ibsen's play in a public theatre in this country; and they returned to sample the Shakespeare. From that date, April 1922, the Old Vic was on its feet.

The first departure from Shakespeare was in December 1921 when *Advent* of August Strindberg was presented. This too I believe was the first production of a Strindberg play to be given in a public theatre in England.

Miss Baylis had never heard of Strindberg but my explanation that the play was a Christmas sermon, told in the 'once upon a time' style, broke down her objections to the departure from the regular fare. The play did not find many friends and when *Peer Gynt* was announced the Old Vic regulars shouted their intention to boycott the production. The Ibsen success made them wish to repent the threat, but many were unable to get to it owing to the heavy bookings by the West End public.

Miss Baylis was not altogether on handshaking terms with Ibsen and only by dangling the bait of the attraction to her opera audience of the Grieg music and that the press might hail her for sowing the seed of making the Old Vic a minor national theatre did I break down her and the Old Vic governors' objections.

William Archer, the translator, made my task of persuasion more difficult by prognosticating failure, owing to the limited technical facilities of the then Old Vic. But no-one was more delighted than he when triumph was achieved. I think Ibsen would have applauded Russell Thorndike's imaginative approach to Peer and the Ase of Florence Buckton; the Dovre King of Andrew Leigh and the Button Moulder of Rupert Harvey were magnificent accomplishments. Hats off too to Charles Corri, the Old Vic's resident conductor. How he loved the change from '*Cav*' and '*Pag*' etc., and cheers too for Wilfrid Walter's designs and painting for the scenes.

The success of *Gynt* whetted my appetite to break the routine now and again, good for me and good for the company. During my five years' stewardship 15 non-Shakespeare plays were presented. One was a yearly fixture, when an Eastertide special matinee of *Everyman* was given.

I had played Death under Ben Greet, but had never seen William Poel's production from whom Greet borrowed a lot. Poel's first production of the old morality was in 1901, in the Master's Court of the Charterhouse, and he was famous overnight. My first presentation was in 1922 and I suggested to Miss Baylis that she invite Mr. Poel to direct it; this he declined, but in gratitude for the help I had given him, he marked my copy of *Everyman* with his tunes, and over many talks mapped out the production. The only lovable argument was over my decision to cast a male for the role of Everyman. Hitherto a female was cast, notably May Douglas Reynolds and Edith Wynne Matthison with Poel and Sybil Thorndike with Greet. I cast Wilfrid Walter and many people liked the change.

In 1922 Massinger's *A New Way to Pay Old Debts* was given, with myself as Sir Giles Overreach. What a part, and what a good play, full of good parts, conventional maybe, yet interesting and lifelike. When as Overreach facing his adversaries, with drawn sword and looking, as one character remarks, ghastly and mad beyond recovery, I attempted Edmund Kean's leap and collapse in the air. E. A. Baughan, reporting in the *Daily News*, wrote that I did not at this point make him faint as Kean is reported to have made Lord Byron, but I did make him 'sit up'. Certain passages in the play have a Shakespearean ring. I loved speaking,

> The garments of her widowhood laid by,
> She now appears as glorious as the spring.

I must record the magnificent performance of Hay Petrie as Greedy.

On 20 February 1924, the Old Vic, as with *Peer Gynt*, again made theatrical history by presenting for the first time to an English audience a faithful version of Goethe's *Faust*, including five scenes from Part II, translated by Graham and Tristan Rawson. Former stage productions had been supplied with an ad hoc version, with no attempt to follow Goethe's scene-division, which is so characteristic of *Faust*.

Irving had his text from Wills, Tree from Stephen Phillips. The *Morning Post* wrote,

Graham and Tristan Rawson have done their work extremely well, their verse being terse and resonant. The house was crowded and one has never known an audience more silently absorbed in what was being said and done on the stage. The reception was equal to any that one has known, even at the Old Vic. *Faust* might prove as remarkable a draw as *Peer Gynt* did last season. The play was admirably acted.

It certainly was, for Ion Swinley as Faust, George Hayes as Mephistopheles, Hay Petrie as the Scholar, John Laurie and Wilfrid Walter as the Angels Michael and Raphael, Jane Bacon and Ethel Harper as Margaret and Martha, all gave performances worthy of any theatre in the world. I agree with the critic of the *Daily Herald*, 22 February 1924, 'A remarkable night'. The press applauded the courage of the effort and praised the accomplishment. Yes, *Faust* was a success and found new friends for the auditorium and consequently for Shakespeare.

As with the Shakespeare, the mounting of *Faust* was simple; it had to be, for shekels for production were hard to come by, since Gounod had to be fed as well as Goethe, and the financial situation was not aided by the L.C.C.'s demand, reconstruct or CLOSE. New timber and canvas were in short supply, but Wilfrid Walter designed and painted a series of scenes that caught the spirit of the play and period, using the backs of old scene cloths and breaking up flats that had been in the building since the time of Queen Victoria.

Both *Gynt* and *Faust* made heavy calls upon the lighting plant, which in the spring of 1924 was, to put it mildly, only adequate. On my takeover in 1920 I had insisted upon the installation of some front of house lighting, but the stage equipment was still poor and under pressure; the switchboard was inclined to burn out. But the handicaps did not daunt one, indeed they spurred the inventive and imaginative senses to such an extent that Mr. Basil Dean, admiring a lighting effect in *Gynt*, was taken aback when I showed him that I was using an electric bulb in a biscuit tin.

The only non-Shakespeare play to benefit by the reconstruction of the theatre was A. W. Pinero's *Trelawny of the 'Wells'* presented in June 1925. In the old theatre the Shakespeare scene was well cared for; on taking office in 1920 I swept aside all ideas of scenic presentation, as practised by my predecessors, and insisted upon the building of a semi-permanent set, obeying the groundplan of the Elizabethan theatre, with inner stage and upper galleries. Some of the governing body of the Vic feared the austerity of my approach to Shakespeare, but Miss Baylis backed me up. If she had faith in a person she would fight, even if she did not quite understand the aim. In spite of the governing body, she was the governor. However, I placated the wavering members by assuring them that the setting allowed for the introduction of the painted inset scene. What really frightened them was my use of a black traverse, hung where the supports of the Heaven might have been, for the front scenes. The playing before the black drop was heightened by the restoration of what S. R. Littlewood, then President of the Critics Circle, termed 'that knobbly piece of oak', the forestage. This allowed the actor to be embraced by occupants of the stage boxes and created a certain intimacy with the entire auditorium, and continuity of action was assured. The shape of the theatre made it impossible to be truly Elizabethan, but the forestage helped rapidity of speech and with staging obeying the author's construction of the plays, it was possible to catch the spirit of Elizabethan presentation.

It was no easy task wooing the Old Vic regulars to recognise the fact that we owe to the absence of painted canvas many of the finest descriptive passages in Shakespeare. He wrote with consummate art to show the tide of human affairs, its flow and ebb, and his construction plan is particularly unsuited to the act-drop. The changeover was drastic and it was perhaps tough on the regulars, asking them to accept, without as it were any 'running in', the sound of words for the painting of a locality, or the actor's description of the sunrise in *Hamlet* in lieu of the facility of an electrician.

It was a tough job for me too, for it was only in the spring of 1918 when I wrote to Miss Baylis from a front line trench, laughingly enclosing my first season's programme, although no invitation had been extended to me to join the Old Vic on my return from the war. But her words and even more her smile, when bidding me a safe return, kept alive a hope that I might be wanted.

Incidentally, the 'trench' programme was strictly adhered to for my first season. I carried a volume of Shakespeare in my knapsack, and at times cursed the weight of it. The poet was eventually dumped, under orders, 40 miles north of Jaffa, I being told by the sergeant that I was there to fight, not to read bloody poetry. He certainly laughed when I said, 'it doesn't matter, most of it is in my head'. Iron rations replaced the poetic weight.

During my apprenticeship to the spectacular, 1906–1909 under Tree at His Majesty's Theatre, protests at the method came from many quarters. A nameless writer in Blackwood's magazine made the broad statement that Shakespeare's plays 'afford no decent opportunity for elaborate scenery and it should be impossible to turn the plays to the vulgar use of stage illusion'.

A heavy storm of protest broke over Tree's production of *Antony and Cleopatra*, presented in December 1906. In his foreword in the printed copy of his stage version, Tree wrote:

In the third act the play presents many difficulties. The action of the drama is switched from Athens to Alexandria with extreme suddenness.

In one scene of the text, Antony is at his city of Athens directing the government of his section of the Roman Empire; in the next we learn, but only through the mouth of Octavius Caesar, that he had departed for Alexandria, and is in the toils of the Egyptian Queen. This transition seems sudden and unexpected to the spectator and to elucidate the position to the audience, the producer has ventured to bridge this gap in the action of the play by presenting in the form of a tableau the incident so vividly described by Shakespeare in the mouth of Octavius Caesar, of Antony's return to Egypt and Egypt's Queen.

The tableau was a magnificent exhibition of stage carpentry, lighting, grouping and movement of people, with much blare of trumpets, banging of drums and waving of banners and shouting of the populace, but the splendour of the intrusion made necessary sacrificing pages of the text. In the book, *Herbert Beerbohm Tree*, Lady Tree refers to her husband's production of the play as 'Put upon the stage with all his glowing sense of gorgeous pageantry', but adds: 'I consider it to have been one of his rare failures.'

The production certainly played into the hands of the anti-spectaculars, 'the adequats' as HBT termed them.

Critics of his production of *The Tempest* had likened him to Charles Kean who had been termed an 'upholsterer', a 'spectacle-maker' and a 'poodle-trimmer'. 'Can,' said Tree, 'the beauties and fantasy of the play be conveyed to the senses of an audience by means of what is called "adequate" treatment?' Chief of the adequats was William Poel, who in 1894 founded the Elizabethan Stage Society and from that date devoted his life to the Elizabethan revival.

I did not meet William Poel till 1919 and in the early stages of my career my knowledge of the Elizabethan theatre was scanty; in fact I knew little or nothing about it, nor did the general public. Publication of research work upon the subject attracted little attention.

The minority attack upon the Irving and Tree tradition received little attention from the public but Poel's experimental performances in theatres, Inns of Court and open spaces, his writings and lectures gave food for thought to many members of the acting profession, and while William Archer severely criticised, and Max Beerbohm ridiculed Poel's efforts, such influential critics as Shaw, Montague, Desmond MacCarthy and Farjeon publicised the importance of what Poel was doing.

Talks with Esmé Percy, who in 1905 had played Romeo for Poel and was an enthusiastic Poelite, sent me in search of matter pertaining to the Elizabethan theatre, and he gave me a bunch of single sheets published by Poel for private circulation among friends. They dealt with the way in which the plays of Shakespeare and the Elizabethan dramatists should be represented on the stage today. Poel's demand was, go to the text, study the period.

In 1906 my ignorance upon the subject was appalling, and as a member of Mr. Tree's company it was little short of blasphemy to back up the 'adequats'; it was shoulder to shoulder, with the slogan: what was good enough for Macready, Irving and Tree is good enough for me. But the seed was sown, and after reading reports and speaking with people who had seen Poel's 1881 performance of *Hamlet* at the St. George's Hall and the 1903 *Measure for Measure* at the Royalty Theatre, converted into as near a resemblance of the old Fortune Playhouse as was possible in a roofed theatre, curiosity deepened, and adherence to the spectacular began to waver.

In 1910, when I was gaining experience under the management of Henry Herbert, who was touring the Benson North company, the influence of Poel was evident, for Poel and Herbert had been co-mates with F. R. Benson's own company. The large-hearted Beerbohm Tree invited Poel to present his Elizabethan performance of *All's Well that Ends Well* during that year's Shakespeare Festival at His Majesty's Theatre. I was able to see it, and it was an eye and ear opener. Gone were the trappings, an apron stage was built over the spacious orchestra pit, and front of house lighting was installed. The background obeyed the construction of Shakespeare's stage, allowing rapid action. Only one interval, and even in that fairly large theatre, intimacy was established between actor and audience. I turned traitor to the spectacular. Tree profited too from Poel's production for he retained the apron and front lighting for his eventual presentation of *Henry VIII*. My few months, during the early period of the 1914 war, at the really dirty Old Vic under the direction of Ben Greet, gave me acting chances and stage managerial experience, but I noted Ben's method was rather slipshod, and though a great friend and follower of Poel, no spirit of Poel existed.

And so when the day came to put on the costume of a soldier, I marched away armed with the text and a firm resolution that if I returned from the war and was invited to control production at the Vic, the spirit of Poel would be my yardstick. And I had not met the man.

I was demobilised in May 1919, and after two weeks of melodrama, *Two Little Vagabonds* and *The Sailor's Wedding* at the Theatre Royal Portsmouth, spent a few weeks with Ben Greet, playing in town halls and open spaces, and then was contracted as walking understudy to Norman McKinnel in *The Voice from the Minaret*, a play by Robert S. Hichens that opened at the Globe Theatre on 26 August 1919. A dreary job, but after three years of soldiering one was lucky to get back to the West End, especially as the provincial theatre was in a parlous state.

During the run the great moment came. William Poel presented himself at the stage door and could I spare him a few moments? I followed the stage door keeper down the stairs, wondering if I had heard aright, and stood before one of the loveliest faces I had ever seen. He would not keep me long, and refusing a sit down for coffee at a cafe, began to pace me up and down on the pavement, telling me that he had watched much of my work with Tree and Greet and had come to the conclusion that my voice would answer to his tunes. Every few words was punctuated by a nervous burrr. He was preparing a vocal recital of *Such Stuff as Dreams Are Made of*, Fitzgerald's translation of Calderon's *La Vida es Sueno*, to be given at the Ethical Church, Bayswater, and he would like me to rehearse an important role. Explaining that he always rehearsed his artists individually for three or four weeks, my first reading was fixed for 3 p.m. at the Browning Rooms, Adelphi, two days later. With a smile so beautiful that it hurt, he thought that we would get on well together, and then with a roguish change of face, 'Some people think I'm mad, perhaps you will too'.

I trod on air as I followed his slightly stoopy figure glide away with the silver hair flowing from under his hat. The many stories of his eccentric behaviour came to my mind and I was an early victim, for meeting him at the place and time appointed for the reading, he had forgotten to book the room; but no matter, for he paced me round the Charing Cross station, sat me down in the waiting room, produced a child's copybook into which he had written my part, sat down beside me, produced his copy of the play, bade me take no notice of anyone, but to recite the lines after him. I opened the play with a four-page non-stop speech, and noted that many words were underlined. They were the key words, to be hit with a high, low or middle tone. The space between the written lines contained upward and downward slanting lines, denoting the tonal approach to the key words; a squiggly line meant, on the level. Poel was quite oblivious to the many people using the waiting room but as my eyes and ears saw and heard what they thought of us, I became nervous and failed to follow his high-pitched and quavering voice. 'Take no notice,' he cried, 'Take no notice, follow me.' Rather difficult, when I heard one man say, in passing, 'a couple of bloody madmen'. The second rehearsal was held in Kensington Gardens, much to the amusement of the many nurse-maids and their charges. How I passed the test under these conditions I do not know, but he was satisfied that I could play his tunes and be of use to him as a stage manager.

Thus began an association that revolutionised my attitude towards Shakespearean presentation. During the weeks of preparation for the Calderon performance, Poel prepared me for my second venture with him, to help stage manage *All's Well that Ends Well*. His close teaching was at times trying, and often one thought he was a little mad; well, he was, but there was a method behind his creating mind. The artists that stood up to the strain of his instruction, and many could not, saw the plays of Shakespeare through Elizabethan eyes. His partiality for females in leading male roles was irritating, but to him they were more obedient to his tunes. It was during quiet conversation that this dedicated man dropped more pearls than during rehearsals, and the following statement from him covers much ground.

> Much depends upon the stage-manager, who must have courage to ignore stage tradition, and imagination to grasp the possibilities of his new freedom. He must look closer to nature than he has been accustomed to do, and must realise that the tableau is replaced by the faces, the voices and the gestures of the actors, who become of vital importance to the audience, as interpreters of the drama. The public has not yet learned to separate the poet's plays from their historical period, or from their foreign locality, and to look at them through Elizabethan spectacles. Nor is Shakespeare's dramatic art yet understood, since hitherto his plays have been forced into a setting for which they were never intended. Without an intimate knowledge of the poet's constructive art for the theatre for which he wrote, it is impossible to hope that the right point of view will be caught with regard to what is, or is not, of importance to accentuate in the story.

He knew that I hoped to go to the Old Vic and was aware of my proposed programme, and gave me much advice, but as one grew to know him one had to be wary and pick the grain from the chaff for he was not altogether consistent; he would lecture on Monday upon the play to be seen on Tuesday, calling down the wrath of God upon any director of a Shakespeare play who transposed a comma, and one was horrified at his mutilation of the text, transposition of scene and here and there the substitution for the poet's text of lines of his own. One forgave him for, in spite of his waywardness and stubbornness, one gathered the principles of the approach to an Elizabethan revival.

Mr. Robert Speaight has, in his splendid book *William Poel and the Elizabethan Revival*, left to posterity a faithful record of Poel's greatness, plus the weaknesses. It is a pity that Poel could never find a theatre in which to establish the open platform with the audience on three sides. His experiments were confined to the proscenium theatre that allowed only a small jut of platform before the background, that gave little freedom to the actors and no idea of Elizabethan intimacy.

But the mind behind pointed the way. I worked with Poel during the autumn of 1919 and spring 1920, and the call from the Old Vic came to take up my duties in the June of that year. Poel advised me to accept. I did not know then that he had urged Miss Baylis to give me a trial. I wavered, doubting if I had picked up sufficient knowledge during the short time I had worked with Poel, to persuade artists to help me in the new approach and find an audience to suffer the hard seats of the Old Vic with less painted canvas to look at, and I hoped more to listen to, for their bottoms would suffer because the intervals would be fewer than they had been used to; also the time for preparation was short and I knew that unless I opened up with a bang, all might be lost. But I said 'yes'.

In June 1920 the old tumbler curtain at the Old Vic fell upon the old order, and in August tableau curtains swung apart, revealing a setting that said, with the voice of Shakespeare and Poel,

> And let us, ciphers to this great accompt,
> On your imaginary forces work.

But to return to the non Bardic productions. In November 1921 *Wat Tyler*, a play by Halcott Glover, was given its first public performance and found favour with the Old Vic audience. Bernard Shaw admired the work and popped in twice to see it, saying laughingly to Miss Baylis and myself, '*you'll* be the National Theatre if we are not careful'.

The author profited by the production in a later version, by widening the scope of the play to include glimpses of the young king, Richard II, absent in the original version.

The performance was graced by a magnificent performance by Ernest Milton of John Ball, and Wilfrid Walter, ideal as Jack Straw, provided a splendid series of scenes, including a most imaginative picture of Old London Bridge. This set always met with applause and each night as the curtain fell upon the mob that fought upon it, the reception warmed the blood. The production strained the purse strings, but its success made Miss Baylis ponder upon the words of GBS.

I walked warily, fearing to tread upon her corns, the 'Opera'. The plays were giving six performances a week to the opera's two, and the plays sustained the house. The reverse would have gladdened her heart, but she was proud of her players; I am sure at times she remembered Grumio's line, 'Why, nothing comes amiss, so money comes withal', hoping that money would one day place the opera where she wished it.

Charles Dickens was sandwiched in with an adaptation of *A Christmas Carol* by Russell Thorndike, and a version of *The Cricket on the Hearth* by my wife.* Molière had a look in with *L'Amour Médecin* under the title of

---

* Mary Sumner. The programme attributes the adaptation to Atkins.

Love is the Best Doctor. Sheridan was represented by *The Rivals*, and Goldsmith with *She Stoops to Conquer*, helped by fine performances by Marie Ney, Ion Swinley and Andrew Leigh.

An appeal to me to produce a modern Nativity play entitled *Hope of the World* was in fact an order, for the author was her spiritual adviser, the Rev. Father Andrew, a man for whom I had a profound respect, though he was no playwright; but he did it, and that's that. It was full of Yea's, Nay's and Verily's. The cast referred to the work as the 'soap of the world'. In March 1923 we staged *Arthur*, a tragedy, a play out of Malory's pages as the author Laurence Binyon described it. It was in verse and written for Sir John and Lady Harvey, but they never produced it. This did not surprise me for with a speaking cast of twenty-nine plus a host of supernumeraries, a demanding scenic display, including barges for Elaine floating down-river to Westminster, and for the sorrowing Queen conveying Arthur to Avalon, it would have taxed the then financial position of the great manager, and I wished Miss Baylis to postpone until the autumn, but for what reason I never knew, it had to be in the spring of 1923.

A feature of the occasion was the incidental music composed by Sir Edward Elgar. Unfortunately the score was never published, and at the end of the run the orchestral parts disappeared. This was my first meeting with Sir Edward and the association ripened into a friendship that lasted to his death. He was an ardent theatre-goer and attended many rehearsals, disclosing himself as a good and at times a severe critic.

He helped me by persuading Binyon to allow my cutting, for the play, containing many moments of great beauty, was overlong and overwritten, and realism had to be sacrificed to allow word images to register. His verse was not very actable, and a long battle scene with much dialogue offered difficulties which I overcame by presenting a series of static figures in combat, silhouetted against the sky, with only the faces of the actors illuminated by a torch concealed in the costume. The trick worked, much to the admiration of many onlookers and the press. I borrowed the idea from Tree's silent battle tableau for *King John*, but without scenery, for I presented *Arthur* in curtains.

I suffered many a qualm during rehearsals, for the augmentation of the acting company was not easy, as the pay was poor and the run for two weeks only, and the costume hire went far beyond the average weekly outlay, but fortunately the regulars liked the offering and the names of Binyon and Elgar attracted newcomers from the world of literature and music.

Yes, we hit the target with as firm a knock as when a vexed Sir Edward broke a baton on the bald head of an instrumentalist during an orchestral rehearsal.

In December 1924 I entered upon a production of William Archer's translation of Gerhart Hauptmann's dream poem, *Hannele*, with a light heart, for I had appeared in the play with Beerbohm Tree at His Majesty's Theatre during the Afternoon Theatre season, when Marie Lohr played Hannele.

The Old Vic's Evelyn Neilson was acclaimed in the role by press and public, as were Ion Swinley, George Hayes, Andrew Leigh and Marie Ney in support. Packed houses welcomed the revival. My vision of the Angelic Host was fiercely attacked by the press; it demanded a nebulous treatment, I gave them what I thought Hannele would describe as angels, complete with wings. The press was fiercely attacked on my behalf by Mrs. Philip Snowden. *Hannele* was a big success, and as a forepiece the revival of the Chester Nativity, 'The Paynters and Glasiers' Play', again found favour as it did in 1923. Sir James Barrie's *Pantaloon* was given as a front piece to the *Comedy of Errors* and somewhere I had to squeeze in Gordon Bottomley's play, *Britain's Daughter*. This gave me little pleasure, for it was not a good play.

Ironically my departure from the Old Vic in 1925 was not as I had hoped it would be, with *Cymbeline* in my pocket, but Sir Arthur Pinero's *Trelawny of the 'Wells'* given in aid of the Sadler's Wells fund. Had *Cymbeline* been the bill I would in two years have produced the thirty-six Folio plays, plus *Pericles*, omitted from the Folio, under one roof.

During 1925 Miss Baylis and myself were not seeing eye to eye. I'm afraid the 'green-eyed monster' entered and she flatly refused me the record.

I had to wait for the Open Air Theatre to make the record, which I still hold in this country. No virtue, but an achievement. *Trelawny* was my first meeting with Sir Arthur since the year* when, as a student at Mr. Tree's Academy, he rehearsed me in one of his plays.

In 1925, at the age of 70, this master of the drama and farce of his period was mentally still very much alive. I studied the play with him from his own prompt book, and he gave me two weeks to knock the company into shape. During the third week he popped in and out to polish up. He was delighted with the cast, whose fears of the stories of his ruthlessness at rehearsals were soon dispersed. The snap of the tongue was still there, but so helpful, as was his touch of forcing home inflections by peering into the face of an artist, his protruding eyebrows, stiff as wire, scratching the forehead of the victim, as he put word for word into the mouth of the actor, with the reiteration of, upward or downward, according to the inflection he demanded. As of old, when standing on stage during rehearsal, the book was held in the right gloved hand, the left, ungloved, placed at the small of the back, and

* *See pp 24–25.*

this organ waggled, slowly or furiously according to his irritation at the artist's antics. But all was done in a fatherly tenderness and affection for the oncoming artists, for Marie Ney gave, to use his own words, as good a performance as he could have wished. Dorice Fordred romped home with Avonia Bunn, myself and Margaret Scudamore appeared as the Telfers, Sir Arthur giving me many touches of the mannerisms of Samuel Phelps upon whom the character was founded. John Garside complained about the 'Cheers' magnificently. Altogether the performance was a great success and I forgave Miss Baylis baulking my *Cymbeline*.

In November 1926 the play was revived at the Globe Theatre, Shaftesbury Avenue, with myself in the same position with Sir Arthur, and again playing Telfer with Margaret Scudamore as Mrs. T and Dorice Fordred as Avonia. The rest of the cast was West End folk, with a star as Trelawny, but the lady was a failure, in fact few of the cast reached the Old Vic standard, with the exception of Leon Quartermaine, who was perfection. Thirty-six plays of Shakespeare, with many repeats including five *Hamlet*s in its entirety, plus seventeen non-Shakespeares, and a generous attention to certain of the operas including the first performance of *Tristan and Isolde* at the Vic was the sum total of my five years with Miss Baylis.

CHAPTER TEN

Robert Atkins and the Open Air Theatre, Regent's Park

BY

J. C. TREWIN

WE know that the theatre was born in the open and by day; Greek drama flowered in fire among the sunlight and marble; medieval moralities took the air on their platform-carts. Now, for half a century in London, we have been grateful to the pastoralists of Regent's Park who have a rich ancestral line; happiest maybe in the ebb of a summer evening when verse rhythms come o'er the ear like the sweet south. ('Sweet sound', if you wish; but some of us stick pedantically to Pope's emendation).

THE THIRTIES

Early in the century there had been Regent's Park performances in what were then the Royal Botanical Gardens. The present theatre, opened in a very different shape from today's, derives from a meeting in 1932 between Sydney Carroll—whose real name was George Frederick Francis Carl White-man—an Australian-born impresario and former drama critic, and Robert Atkins, the sole living director who had staged in London practically every play of Shakespeare. One might have thought them an incompatible pair. Atkins was stocky, resolute, slow-spoken, with a voice (imitated by any player who had worked with him) that someone said was like practice for the Last Trump. He was also the affectionate subject of more stories than anybody in the English theatre since Beerbohm Tree, with whom he had worked in youth. After a tough Australian boyhood, Carroll—the name he finally chose; he called himself Frederick Carl at first—came to England when he was eighteen, acted small parts with Wilson Barrett, went success-fully into publishing, wrote drama criticism, and presently, though his assets could be doubtful, tried his hand at management.

When, at length, he aimed at the Open Air he discovered a financial partner in Lewis Schaverien and a vastly experienced director in Atkins, formerly and redoubtably at the Old Vic in the fighting days of Baylis. They began, after grudging permission from the Ministry of Works, with the transference to Regent's Park, for a group of matinees, of the splendid 'black-and-white' *Twelfth Night*, then at the New Theatre, now re-named the Albery. In a performance vocally and visually elegant—Jean Forbes-Robertson as a Viola gravely wistful, and Phyllis Neilson-Terry as an Olivia permitted naughtily to sing the last verse of Feste's farewell—it managed to survive, on all four afternoons, the rain that, according to legend and Feste's song, raineth every day. Certainly, during the summer months of the Thirties and Forties it could rain hard enough. There were only two fine premières in the first sixteen years of the Open Air Theatre; but, as Atkins observed with his booming optimism, that was the luck of the calendar. The Park did have an exceedingly uncomfortable marquee for nights that, otherwise, would have been hopeless. Players disliked the restricted stage after the wide open spaces outside. There could be awkward moments as when, with audience and cast hurried indoors during a sharp downpour, Helena of *A Midsummer Night's Dream* (Martita Hunt), whom no one had told to move, appeared solitary on the greenward. Her voice was heard drifting into the tent: 'O weary night... Where *is* everybody?'

All of this was some distance from 1982. Carroll lost £560 during the *Twelfth Night* trial. No matter: in the summer of 1933 the Open Air Theatre, as a rule called embracingly 'Regent's Park', opened its first full season in Queen Mary's Gardens, its stage and auditorium established then as they would be through nearly three decades: an immense semi-circular sweep of seating, deck-chairs in front, slatted park chairs behind, facing a lawn-stage that was eighty feet long (twice the width of Drury Lane's) and generally unadorned between the flanking bushes. It was backed by a screen of poplar, sycamore, and hazel. Sunk between the front row of deck-chairs and the rim of the stage, behind a privet hedge that masked the footlight floods, was a pit for the prompter—a useful functionary not often troubled.

Many London playgoers took immediately to the theatre, especially on nights of late summer, the stage a shining floodlit panel, trees shadowy behind it, and no mouse stirring. Imagination responded: soon the trees, the bushes, the grass prairie, might have been any conventional theatre, though there were always a few critics to disagree. 'George Warrington' (*Country Life*) was one. Actually James Agate under one of his several pseudonyms, he said testily that he liked lighting, mistrusted Nature's vagaries, preferred a stall to a deck-chair, and (capriciously) loved the glimpse of a prompter in the wings. Luckily, Agate under any name was seldom as influential as he hoped.

From the first the Park was not designed for niggling production, for nervous dabs at the text. Atkins, accepting the fact that any normal problem was doubled in the open air, and especially in this huge arena, saw that his productions had the breadth of style, the broad definite movements, the lucid speech, that could sometimes alarm players keyed to the current naturalistic throw-away. Still, his companies could cope. *Twelfth Night*, which began the season of 1933 on a hot-plate afternoon—one of the luckiest—before an audience of between three and four thousand, had Margaretta Scott and Phyllis Neilson-Terry to alternate Viola and Olivia; Nigel Playfair—who had acted in Regent's Park thirty years earlier, as Malvolio; Atkins himself as Sir Toby, and Leslie French as Feste. Later, Phyllis Neilson-Terry was Rosalind (to the Orlando of Jack Hawkins), and George Grossmith—unaccustomed to Shakespeare—an angular, mannered Touchstone. *A Midsummer Night's Dream*, seldom without the poet-dramatist, Clifford Bax, in his deck-chair on the right of the first row of the central block, proved at once that it would be the most-loved Regent's play through half a century; it could defy choral sparrows, any form of sneaping wind, and ultimately the zooming of aircraft. Towards the close of the season, among a décor of rock pinnacles, palm trees, and exotic flowers, Atkins played in *The Tempest* his famous Caliban, a monster seeking desperately for speech, his intellect dawning like a sullen daybreak. Leslie French's Ariel was the soul of grace (in the *Dream* he had been a definitive Puck). As Prospero, John Drinkwater, sadly under-valued as poet, dramatist, biographer, and actor, employed—sometimes too slowly—his magnificent voice and the large effects that trooped with majesty.

It was an exhilarating season, drawing audiences of over a quarter of a million. Even so, it lost nearly £3,000. Carroll, good theatre-man, was hardly economical. Moreover, he had had to pay a good deal to shape the theatre; the digging-up and transplanting of trees, and the need to ensure that his 'greensward', as the stage was always known, was kept well-drained and springy. The Park in those days had a Master of the Greensward, the veteran Sir Philip Ben Greet, who would appear, superfluously but avuncularly, before every play to welcome the audience and say something about the weather. Shakespeare was not alone. Carroll had begun to include ballets (*Acis and Galatea* for one), and he had an exquisite *première danseuse* in the Danish Nini Theilade. (A young Australian, Robert Helpmann, came to the Park for a season). In 1934 Atkins directed the grave oak-and-crystal beauty of Milton's masque of *Comus* which he repeated three times during the decade: it is remembered now especially for Leslie French's movement and speech as the Attendant Spirit: 'Sabrina fair, /Listen where thou are sitting/ Under the glassy, cool, translucent wave'.

During 1944 Atkins was appointed director of productions at the Shakespeare Memorial Theatre, Stratford-upon-Avon, a thoroughly ungrateful post which he held for two complicated seasons. He did not forget the Park. There, in the summer of 1944, Stephen Thomas put on *The Winter's Tale* (which had been touring), Ernest Milton unremittingly intense as Leontes racked by jealousy's yellow fever, Cicely Byrne as Hermione, and Vivienne Bennett as Paulina. In a *Twelfth Night* (Thea Holme as Viola) Ernest Thesiger, the Malvolio, would have his sole Open Air part, a Grey Eminence who looked at Feste with the expression of a surrealist painter examining the works of Lord Leighton.

At last in 1945, the Park, with Eric Capon as temporary director, began to return more or less to itself with an *As You Like It* that had George Hayes as its Jaques, professional melancholic, and a *Merchant of Venice* (Hayes as Shylock). Next year, free of the Stratford weight, Atkins was back: *As You Like It* and *A Midsummer Night's Dream*, both directed in a style that had become traditional (Atkins with his sunrise restored to him); but also, and surprisingly, *Troilus and Cressida*. Chances to see it in those days were so few that it would have been ungenerous not to applaud Atkins's bravery in raising Troy upon a grassy bank. Audiences were hard to get into the Park habit again; those that ventured were fortunate to have John Byron—who had been the last Stratford Hamlet—to express the rapture and the woe of Troilus, ever likely to strike off such a phrase as 'single famish'd kiss,/Distasted with the salt of broken tears'. Atkins kept going, though now he had to endure—not often visible to the naked eye, Thesiger had said—dreary swathes of empty seats at the back of the huge auditorium. For all that, he would put on, when he could, an Open Air rarity to balance the expected plays. During 1948 he did *King John* (a young man, John Neville, in the few lines of the ambassador, Chatillon), and at midsummer 1949 a determined, if not very fortunate, double bill of conflations of *The Comedy of Errors* and *The Two Gentlemen of Verona*.

A. P. Herbert, in 1948, had written a sonnet to Atkins for the end of *As You Like It*:

> King of all optimists, one more you bare
> Your gallant breast to our rough open air;
> And surely Fate will say that you are right:
> Look!—the barometer went up last night

Very well; but within precisely a month the company had shifted to the marquee. Nothing was predictable. If the main news of 1949 would be the Ministry's belatedly hospitable provision of brick dressing-rooms, and of a new tent for rainy days, these happened to coincide with a particularly good summer.

THE FIFTIES

It followed that the season of 1950, beginning reasonably with *The Winter's Tale* (Anthony Eustrel and Ruth Lodge), could hardly have been worse. As the decade proceeded, with one or two bold choices (*Cymbeline*, and Mary Kerridge's Imogen, in 1952), Atkins found the OAT finances uncommonly glum: 1953 especially *Twelfth Night*—'This is the air, this is the glorious sun'—had to open under canvas. Owing to lack of money, the programme was cut six weeks early, and in 1954 the Park did not open at all, something that bred the expected jeremiads. Then in 1955, Atkins's golden jubilee on the stage, life flourished once more. David William, rising as actor and director, came this year to direct *The Tempest*, with Robert Eddison's commanding Prospero. And in 1956 the important matter was not so much in Regent's Park as at the Baalbek Festival where the company had been invited to play *Hamlet* (Bernard Brown as the Prince) and *Twelfth Night* (Atkins as Toby). It proved to be an immense success under the Lebanese moon, and the director, in the last exciting moments of his long stage life, received the Order of the Cedar.

CHAPTER ELEVEN

Year of Jubilee

So we come again to a day in January. It was on the morning of 26 January 1956, that a golden flutter of greetings telegrams reminded me, with a certain bitter-sweetness, that I had completed fifty years of work in the British theatre. It did not seem so very long since that night of 25 January, in the Edwardian heyday, when I had walked on in *Nero*; that night when the sky-borne meteor fizzled into a squib, and Imperial Rome exploded in the face of Herbert Tree. But the messages told me how far I had gone in half a century; I will not compare myself either to meteor or squib.

It was a moving experience to read these telegrams in the tired light of a winter morning. They came to my Regent's Park flat from all ranks of the profession. If I can quote one here, I choose the message from the Critics' Circle, an affectionate wave from stalls to stage:

> The Critics' Circle sends warmest congratulations as you celebrate your golden jubilee on the stage and wishes you many more years of fine service to Shakespeare.

Later in the year, now on a summer's day, 10 August, more telegrams reminded me that I was seventy: perhaps a less cheerful anniversary, though for me sixty-nine had slipped without a jar into the Psalmist's span. True, I daresay your very young actors, asked to represent a man of seventy, would have appeared bent double, with faces looking like an agonised Clapham Junction, and voices that piped and whistled in the sound. The years grow on one unconsciously; it is hard for a young man to persuade himself that seventy is possible, and too often he shows his incredulity in his make-up.

Both jubilee and birthday meant appearances on sound radio and television. On each occasion I was asked to compare the theatres of the past and present; and each time I had to parry this with the reply, 'When you are celebrating, you do not criticise'. Still, I could not resist a word on Shakespearean speech. With one or two exceptions, Shakespeare, as poet and prose writer, comes off badly in performance. And why? Simply, I suggested, because our drama schools train their students from the wrong end. 'Train from the classics downward' said Dame Madge Kendal. She knew.

I had one alarming jubilee night. Commercial television managed cunningly to link my fiftieth year on the stage with a programme that celebrated the rise of the Café Royal. The link seemed to me to be slender, but there it was: I can hardly say that I enjoyed the night, even if viewers told me that I came through it very well. The idea was simple. I represented the Past. As the Café's famous Domino Room had long been modernised, the cameras had to discover me in the Gilt Room, now the oldest part of the building. There I sat self-consciously at a marble-topped, gilt-legged table, a George Moore cloak wrapped round me, a cigar in my mouth, in my hand a goblet of brandy, and a bottle of it on the table beside my opera hat. If ever I had felt like singing the old song, 'Tableau vivant, there's a picture for you', this was the time.

Fortunately, no-one asked me to sing. The commentator, a charming fellow in modern dinner jacket, described the gilt and mirrored room, and then advanced on me with a puzzled 'Good evening, sir'. I replied, according to my text, 'Good evening. I've just dropped in from the Empire for a spot of food'.

'Did you enjoy the film?'

'Film!' I thundered. 'I mean the Empire Music Hall—the Empire in Leicester Square. Dammit, man, I've just seen the ballet there—Genée—at the Empire.'

He studied me sadly. By this time, I gathered, any listener would be regarding me as a mild eccentric. Opinion must have hardened when I complained that the price of brandy had gone up to fourpence a nip.

In my angry protest at this, my cloak fell off. The commentator explained, 'Good Lord, it's Robert Atkins of the Open Air Theatre!' Turning to the cameras, he introduced me, with terrifying aplomb, as 'that famous actor and Shakespearean *author*.' I could do nothing but gasp; but as soon as the cameras had trundled past me, I swallowed a large whisky and fled.

Yes, an odd night; and yet when I was walking in Regent's Park on the Sunday morning, many people stopped me to say how much they had enjoyed my appearance in the Café Royal. Television, in a few years, has become the most fantastic of all advertising agents.

[*The 1956 season at Regent's Park was buffeted by bad weather and had to close early on 4 August. But compensation was provided in the form of an invitation to take a company out to Lebanon and perform in the Graeco-Roman amphitheatre at Baalbek. This visit was sponsored by Middle East Airlines, and in March Atkins flew out on a reconnaissance.*]

The site resembles that of the Acropolis of Athens. There are acres of ruins, and the resident guide—I sympathised with him—was dejected to know that we could not wait to hear him lecture on the beauties and splendours of entablature, cornice, and scroll. My immediate interest was theatrical, not antiquarian; and we had to get back to Beirut for an appointment with President Chamoun.

I could not see real hope in the high space where the Great Court and the Temple of Jupiter had stood. My friends were surprised. A French company, they said, meant to act upon the ruins of the flight of steps that climbed steeply towards the Temple.

'The French company may,' I said, 'but I am bringing actors—not goats and monkeys.'

'Don't bring *Othello!*' at once exclaimed Mr. Alexander, of the British Council.

Why not (it was now suggested) use the orchestral platform to be built over the space between the Temple of Bacchus and the magnificent columns of Jupiter, a space littered with rubble? I was firm. There it would be necessary to use microphones. I was having no more of these. We moved on to the Hexagon Court, and there indeed my Elizabethan spirits cried out. Any hexagonal building invited me, and though little of this was left standing, what did remain upright suggested Shakespeare's stage and auditorium. I became so enthusiastic that Alexander, who remembered my work at the Ring, Blackfriars, had to explain why to a tolerant Mrs. Es-Said.

There was still one more site: the Temple of Bacchus. The moment we entered it I knew that if ever a building called for *Julius Caesar* to be acted within it, this was the place. Tree would not have hesitated. But I had to look at it with one suspicious and one dropping eye. My company would be small. To do *Caesar* at it should be done in the Temple, at least one hundred actors must swarm across the noble range of steps, sixty-five feet wide, that rise from the floor two-thirds of the way to the auditorium.

Normally I am opposed to playing Shakespeare on steps. But here, midway, a platform broke the flight. There was acting space on another wide platform at the top, and the arrangement of columns gave room for an inner stage with appropriate entrances. We could seat an audience of at least a thousand. It would be rather like playing in a baronial hall, ancient and roofless. At once I thought of the production as 'Romobaronial'. Acoustically, the Temple was excellent; I proved this during an extempore recital, much applauded (I was relieved to hear) by a large group of tourists from the Jordan.

[*After various suggestions and counter-suggestions (*Julius Caesar, The Tempest, *a play by Shaw, a modern play), Hamlet and* Twelfth Night *were selected.* Twelfth Night *was in the Regent's Park programme, and the early*

termination of the season afforded a chance to rehearse Hamlet *adequately.
Bernard Brown, who had played Orlando and other parts that year, was cast
as Hamlet.*]

Not only Brown but I went through hell during the *Hamlet* rehearsals. Had
I made a mistake? One day, no, another day, yes, he became pale-visaged as
the days passed, but bless the boy, he was not palehearted. He stood up to my
loving denunciation and accepted words of praise with a grateful smile.

I capped the recital of the story of Arthur Collins who, rehearsing that well
graced actor Iran Berlin in a Jewish role, suddenly shouted, 'Iran, I want less
Berlin and more Jerusalem', with 'Bernard, I want less Brown and more of
Shakespeare's *Hamlet*.'

Sense of rhythm and phrasing was good, but the key words meant nothing
and had to be dug out with at times painful reiteration. Despite his many
terms at a drama school and a varied repertory experience we were fighting
an insufficient technical foundation. Also apparent was a mind preoccupied
with self, and often I had to remind him that when not soliloquising there
were other characters on the scene. When wasting precious time over the
query of Hamlet's madness, I made up *my* mind for him and damned the
commentators. During an after rehearsal talk, over a well earned drink on
both sides, he raised the question of how much an actor should feel during a
performance. I reminded him that Irving contended that the actor felt and
Coquelin that the actor only simulated feeling and that Lord Byron had
written

...in spite of criticising elves.
Those who'd make others feel must feel themselves.

and added Dame Madge Kendal's reminder to an audience she was
addressing, 'That the word "art" is written at the end of the word
"heart". It therefore seems to me that both heart and art must be embodied
by the actor if he is to sway his audience.'

I confessed to being a betwixt and between on the subject but urged a
physical and vocal control. If you have too much natural feeling, technique
can save an audience many an embarrassing moment; if true feeling is
limited, technique can gull the public. To add to the ham-damning at
rehearsals, I gave him daily periods of callisthenics, under the care of the
'open air' choreographer, Miss Stephenson, and towards the end of the
London rehearsals his natural qualities began to emerge and a Hamlet
took life. He was speaking the verse with 'good accent and good dis-
cretion' and marking the change into prose. Loving insinuations were
breathed into his ears up to the last moment of rehearsal in the Temple

and I left him to his fate with one fear that when before the public he might go berserk; but no, his final bow was to a storm of sincere applause for a performance of a Hamlet, and the Lebanese are not fools. My bag of Hamlets, having seen them, played with, or produced them is 36 and Bernard Brown is well away from the bottom in order of merit.

On the day of our arrival at Beirut a daily paper flashed a headline, 'Britons in Lebanon told to Pack', but our reception at the airport belied the instructions, for the welcome from members of the festival committee, headed by their President Mrs. Charles Kettaneh and by now my dear friend Mrs. Es-Said, was warm with sincere friendship. Mr. Raymond Gauntlett, representing the British Ambassador, told me quietly that the Lebanese interest in the British troupe far exceeded their interest in the German and French contingents who had completed their seasons. I did not know till success crowned our efforts that the British officials and residents predicted a flop for us.

We touched down at Beirut at 10 p.m., and after the reception a fleet of cars whirled us over the mountains to Baalbek. It was a drive through fairyland for the people of Beirut were dwelling in the mountains to escape the heat of the coastline and the many townships, hamlets and palatial residents from miles around twinkled their lights.

Early next morning, standing with my wife on the balcony of our room in the Palmyra Hotel where the company was housed, we gazed upon an azure sky and felt a heat that boded to melt the six columns of Jupiter that bowed to us through the poplar-strewn ground that lay between the hotel and the acres of ruins. Below the columns the limestone walls of the Temple of Bacchus glinted a welcome through the trees. I felt that the walls held a secret; would we be successful? Beyond, a flank of the Lebanon ranges rolled and jagged to the sky, and above all the sun, that never fails to shine upon the Lebanon from May to November, gave me some comfort; success or no, no rain would fall upon the roofless Temple of Thespi—I beg its pardon, Bacchus.

In spite of the heat, intensive rehearsal was the order of the day and it became a case of changing Noel Coward's wording to 'Mad dogs and Englishmen rehearse in the midday sun'. Comfort came from vendor Moses who fortified us with iced lemonade in earthen beakers. The company, bless them, stood up to it to a man and woman, even postponing their tummy troubles until the last performance was given. We left no stone or step unturned, to give of our best. At times, during rehearsals, tourists from Jordan or Syria would invade the pro tempore privacy of the Temple, and armed police would order them out, but I said no, 'the twain *shall* meet' and during let-ups the company and the people of the east made friends.

The members of the festival committee did all in their power for our comfort and happiness and the people of Baalbek, from the butcher carving up his scraggy meat to the gabardined maker of chairs, breathed kindness. I owe much to Nayib Y. Najjar, deputed by the Sheikh Najib as liaison officer, for he came to my rescue to repair the omission of Azzi: no screens, furniture or shrubs in tubs had been collected. The latter came through Mrs. Es-Said, and she presented me with 25 beautiful shrubs in tubs, the like of which Regent's Park has never seen. I dubbed her 'My Lady of the Shrubs'.

I saw the sun rise on Saturday 25 August 1956, not because I wished to witness the spectacle, for spectacle it was, but anxiety interfered with sleep, and I remembered the many times I had, during my service in the 1914 war, seen the hills of Palestine tinged with the promise of a broiling day. And then my thoughts recalled the Cairo of 1927–8, when as the guest of the Egyptian government I had presented seasons of Shakespeare, and on each occasion *Hamlet* was the opening play, and triumphed. I prayed for success among these friendly people of the Lebanon, although many of them had approved of Nasser's action in seizing the canal.

At a before-the-play cocktail party given by the British Ambassador in the lovely grounds of the Kawahm Hotel, I was surprised and more than delighted to find the deus ex machina of the season, Sir Francis Brake. He had found time to fly from London. Mr. Basil Smallpiece, managing director of BOAC, was with him. The Temple was filled to capacity, headed by the President of the Lebanon and the British and Syrian ambassadors, complete with entourage. The general audience was mainly Arabic, from Syria and Jordan as well as the Lebanon, mixed with French, English and American. Many of them had travelled two and three hundred miles. I found a vantage point for watching the stage and audience, hard by an exit through which I could escape if my nerves got the better of me.

I made a few escapes and stood within hearing of what was happening inside, only half sensing the grandeur and majesty of the moonlit columns of Jupiter. Laughter from within, resulting from Russell Thorndike's magnificent performance of Polonius, and loud applause on a Hamlet exit, was balm to my ears and then I wondered, would the God of the columns attempt to wreak vengeance on the prancing figures in Elizabethan costumes for desecrating the steps on which his priests in sacerdotal dress were wont to perform religious ceremonies?

I returned to the auditorium and was staggered. What had happened to the lighting? I swore vengeance on the electrical staff, but on looking skyward realised that the full moon was enjoying the performance and that till she went on her way human efforts were outshone.

At the first interval reports were more than favourable. At the second interval I was taken by Azzi, who whispered something into my ear about a decoration, to the President's 'box', a wooden balcony erected at the back of the Temple. His Excellency Camille Chamoun, a magnificent figure of a man, tall, broad shouldered with a face of great strength and beauty, shook me warmly by the hand and showered congratulations, as did his gracious wife. The British Ambassador beamed upon me and whispered, 'your triumph will help me tremendously'. The sincerity of the congratulations made me feel that we were winning through and, armed with a glass of champagne, began a retreat, to be faced by Sir Francis Brake who, gripping me by the hand said, 'Atkins, I'm proud of you and England should be too'. This took me down the steps, to be arrested by Azzi who told me to stay put.

The audience having re-assembled, the President cocked a finger toward me and bade me follow him, and when upon the stage, after a short speech he pinned upon my breast the Order of the Cedar. The audience shouted their approval and my reply seemed to please them. Asking Sir Francis if I had said the right things, he said 'no politicians could have equalled you'.

At the end of the performance the company received a tumultuous reception, and a very happy and excited company gathered on the Sunday morning for the final rehearsal of *Twelfth Night*, to be performed in the evening.

The shrubs made a gallant showing, the steps assuming the look of an Italian garden. The performance of *Hamlet* removed all doubts about a language barrier and I felt sure that the romantic side of the comedy would get over, though I was dubious towards the humour; but my fears were groundless for the Captain's line, 'What great ones do the less will prattle at' was received with a quiet ripple of laughter, and legitimate laughter followed lines that 'never get a titter' at home.

For the first time in my many productions of *Twelfth Night* I dispensed with a table and chairs for the well-known kitchen scene, fearing they would prove an anachronism in the austere setting, and caroused and plotted with Aguecheek and Maria sitting on the Temple steps.

An American critic wrote, 'Robert Atkins as Sir Toby Belch was the hit of the evening, considered by many as the perfect drunk, the natural drunk, really an authentic drunk and the funniest drunk as well as all these together. It was a beautiful piece of acting'. It was a joyous evening and we received a joyous acclamation, if anything more tumultuous than for *Hamlet*, but I think it was that many of the Americans, having seen the Tragedy, were thanking us for both plays. A repeat of *Hamlet* on the Monday, again played to a capacity house, brought the festival to a close and it was voted on all sides that the English troupe was the highlight of the 1956 Baalbek Festival.

It would be invidious to show favour in a company that so worthily upheld the honour of English acting, but I am sure that Miss Patricia Kneale, Miss Rosemary Wallace, Mr. Bernard Brown, Mr. Russell Thorndike and Mr. Alan Judd will always remember with warm pleasure the many compliments paid to their beautiful performances by the people of the Lebanon. I can pick out the staff, for the stage manager, Miss Barnard, and Miss Shirley Evans, mistress of the wardrobe, worked wonders under conditions that made me forgive pausings in their labours 'to cleave the air with horrid speech', for dressing accommodation, space for properties and wardrobe was in a crypt, deep in the bowels of the earth where the priests were wont to keep their ceremonial and sacerdotal gear.

Hamlet and Sir Toby Belch shared a space behind a screen on the stage with a most ancient block of stone as a table and a kerosene lamp for light. I am sure that the priests of the BC period had better lavatory arrangements. The festival committee were aware and sensitive to the inconveniences, but the happy company like good troupers made light of the situation.

Their labours were rewarded with four days' rest at the Palm Beach Hotel in Beirut as guests of the Lebanon government, during which the bathing and local sightseeing was punctuated daily by 20, 30 and 40 mile drives into the mountains for luncheon, dinner or cocktail parties in the lovely summer homes of members of the committee. The Lebanon is a lovely country and its people have a burning desire for friendship with Britain. There is no theatre there and it is hoped that the annual festival will develop the need.

And so back to England, to the rain, Grays Inn and the Masque.

GRAYS INN

The actual date of the founding of our Court of Graya is unknown, but the archives show that it was functioning in 1311. After Drake had vanquished the Spanish Armada the screen installed in the Great Hall of the Sun was carved from timbers of the Spanish fleet. One third of the magnificent screen, and the pictures and stained glass windows, providently stored away, was all that remained of the hall after the 'airy devils' of Germany wreaked their vengeance on the city of London in 1941.

The very faithful reconstruction of the hall is a lasting tribute to the architects concerned and when a few years have mellowed the stone and wood the smell of Tudor, Elizabethan and Stuart revelling will ooze from the hammer-beams.

The Lord of Misrule for 1956 was not granted as full a licence for revelling with gentlewomen as was his predecessors, for a royal bencher hoped we would not 'Rock 'n Roll'. We did not, and were mindful of a line in Lady Bacon's letter, written in 1594 to her son Anthony, 'I trust they will not mum nor mask nor sinfully revel at Gray's Inn.'

Of two things I am certain; Queen Bess never looked upon a more graceful and comely group of ladies in waiting as represented by lady members of Gray's Inn 1956. They wore the Elizabethan fashions with ease and dignity and in the high lavolta performed 'Aloftie jumping or a leaping around' with the allowed abandon; and that no mummers of Gloriana's time were more gloriously banqueted than were the mummers of 1956.

To reconstruct the entertainment given at Gray's Inn in 1594 was one thing, and the presentation of the Masque contained in the Gesta Grayorum was another, for the latter was played before Queen Bess at the Royal Court, Whitehall, at Shrovetide. My job was to combine the two events.

From
Gesta Grayorum
or, The
History
of the
Prince of Purpoole,
Anno Domini, 1594

The great number of gallant Gentlemen that Grays-Inn afforded at ordinary Revels, betwixt All-hallentide and Christmas, exceeding therein the rest of the Houses of Court, gave occasion to some well-willers of our sports, and favourers of our credit, to wish a head answerable to so noble a body, and a leader to so gallant a company: which motion was more willingly hearkened unto, in regard that such Pass-times had been intermitted by the space of three or four years, by reason of sickness and discontinuances. After many consultations had hereupon, by the youths, and others that were most forward herein, at length, about the 12th of December, with the consent and assistance of the readers and ancients, it was determined that there should be elected a Prince of Purpoole, to govern our state for the time; which was intended to be for the credit of Grays Inn, and rather to be performed by witty inventions, than chargeable expenses. Where-upon, presently they made choice of one Mr. Henry Helmes, a Norfolk-gentleman, who was thought to be accomplished with all good parts, fit for so great a Dignity; and was also a very proper Man of Personage, and very active in dancing and revelling.

This gave me the idea for the first movement of the entertainment which was the mock ceremonial of the 'Inthorization of the Prince of Purpoole', I was rather staggered to discover that the Prince's retinue numbered some two hundred persons, but fifty modern Griffyns made a fine showing in their doublet and hose, and Mr. Peter Street, a member of my Park and Lebanon company, caused much amusement by his fine declamation in hailing the Inthroned Prince, well represented by Mr. Lush, a member of the Inn.

> To Henry, the most illustrious and most Puissant Prince Purpoole, Archduke of Stapulia and Bernardia, Duke of High and Nether Holborn, Marquis of St. Giles and Tottenham, Court Palatine of Bloomsbury and Clerkenwell, Great Lord of the Cantons of Islington, Kentish Town, Paddington and Knightsbridge, Knight of the most Heroical Order of the Helmet and most serene Sovereign of the same. Relying upon the affability by which mighty princes are ever distinguished, may I be permitted to express to your Highness the good will of our muse, and in the presence of these gentlemen, to convey to you my humble congratulations upon your splendid triumphant and world renowned return from Russia.

The Masque that followed is the story of 'Proteus and the Adamantine Rock', regarded by Enid Welsford in her masterly work *The Elizabethan Masque* as a 'turning point in the history of the masque, being the first piece that we know of which gives the norm of the masque as composed by Ben Jonson and his fellow poets'. Unlike the Jonson-Inigo Jones combinations, not in their stride in 1594, the Gesta Grayorum did not give scope for much disguisings, elaborate scenery or machines. The directions in Gesta Grayorum were:

The Speakers

An Esquire of the Princes Company, attended by a Tartarian Page.
Proteus, the Sea-God, attended by two Tritons.
Thamesis and Amphitrite, who likewise were attended by their Sea Nymphs.
These five were Musicians which sung on the first coming on the stage.
At the first coming on the stage, the Nymphs and Tritons sung this Hymn following, in praise of Neptune; which being ended, the speakers made their speeches in order as followeth.

Then were set down the two verses of the Hymn to Neptune followed by the set speeches for the Esquire and Proteus. It is supposed that Campion penned the Hymn to Neptune and Davison the set speeches, but unlike Ben Jonson, these gentlemen admitted no 'stage directions' into the text, and the speeches numbered only 276 lines.

129

So my *Love's Labour* was to emulate Ovidius Naso and 'Smell out the odoriferous flowers of fancy, the jerks of invention'. Jerk number one was to ask my friend Clifford Bax to write a prologue and his nimble brain produced eighteen lines of most delicate fancy. I jerked in a Jester and swelled the Court of Proteus with extra Tritons, Nymphs and added porpoises. The followers of Proteus and the seven Knights attending the Prince of Purpoole were professional dancers, and magnificently did the arranger, Miss Geraldine Stephenson, handle the interspersed dances, all to a true Elizabethan measure, and the music composed by Mr. John Dalby never betrayed the period.

The musicians and singers, situated in the musicians' gallery above the scene, made a gallant show in their red gowns and white ruffs. An interpolation that was much enjoyed was the representation by Mr. Gordon Honey of Robert Hales, a favourite singer of Elizabeth I, singing her favourite song, accompanied most beautifully by lutenist Miss Diana Poulton.

I was brave enough to direct Honey to sing the last verse sitting at the Queen's feet on the dais. The Lord Burghley and Sir Francis Bacon looked from their frames upon their modern representations in the persons of S. Parnell Kerr and Charles Burke, and Elizabeth I, gazing over the head of Elizabeth II as she sat in her chair of state made specially for the occasion, saw the Lord Thomas Havard, the Earl of Southampton, Sir Thomas Heneage and his Lady.

These people of quality were represented by members of the Inn, their dialogue being written by me. Robert Speaight and Dennis Chinnery as the Esquire and Proteus delivered the difficult speeches with gallantry, charm and humour, Speaight being magnificently effective in the usual direct address to the Queen:

> Excellent Queen, true Adamant of Hearts;
> Out of that sacred Garland ever grew
> Garlands of Vertues, Beauties and Perfections,
> That crowns your Crown, and dims your Fortune's Beams,
> Vouchsafe some Branch, some precious flower or leaf,
> Which, though it wither in my barren Verse,
> May yet suffice to over-shade and drown
> The Rocks admired of this Deny-God.

The compiler of Gesta Grayorum gave me a clue for the end of the Masque and a lead into the Revels for he noted:

> When these speeches were thus delivered, Proteus with his trident
> striking of Adamant, which was mentioned in the speeches, made

utterance for the Prince and his seven Knights, who had given themselves as hostages for the performance of the Covenants between the Prince and Proteus, as is declared in the speeches. Hereat Proteus, Amphitrite and Thamesis, with their attendants, the Nymphs and Tritons, went into the Rock and then the Prince and the seven Knights issued forth of the Rock, in a very stately Mask, very richly attired, and gallantly provided of all things meet for the performance of so great an enterprise. At their first coming on the stage, they danced a new devised Measure, etc. After which they took unto them ladies; and with them they danced their Galliards, Courants etc. and they danced another new measure.

The finale of the Revel, a clever suggestion by Sir Leonard Stone, was the mock death of the Jester, and on his final contortion, a pause, my voice rang out:

'Misrule is ended.'

A roll on the drums, and the national anthem. The performance was played on the floor of the hall, entrance being through the right and left doorways of the screen. The audience occupied the three sides and crowded into what space was left in the musicians' gallery.

Her Majesty the Queen, the Duke and Duchess of Gloucester, the Duchess of Devonshire, the Lord Chancellor and Lady Kilmuir, Sir Leonard Stone and other glittering notabilities faced the players. On presentation Her Majesty expressed gracious appreciation and it was my honour to present the players, with whom Her Majesty held individual and animated conversation. One felt that Her Majesty had read the closing lines of Gesta Grayorum:

> For the present Her Majesty graced every one; particularly, she thanked His Highness for the good performance of all that was done; and wished that their Sports had continued longer, for the pleasure she took therein; which may well appear, by her answer to the Courtiers who danced a Measure immediately after the Mask was ended; saying, What Shall we have Bread and Cheese after a Banquet? And Her Majesty gave them her hand to kiss, with most gracious words of commendations to them; particularly and in general, of Grays Inn as an house that she was much beholden unto, for that it did always study for some Sports to present unto her.

The Under Treasurer, Mr. Oswald Terry, whose devotion during the days of preparation did not belie his nickname, 'The Wizard of Os', saw to it that

'Bread and Cheese' was not the order of the night, and the 'Sports' presented on 13 November 1956 was the first entertainment there attended by a British reigning monarch since the days of Charles II, for no occupant of our throne had crossed the threshold of the Inn during the years between, and Grayans are under a heavy debt to the Treasurer, Sir Leonard Stone, who during his term of office caused the Royal presence, and I thank him for giving me a Royal and Glorious finale to my year of Jubilee.

TWELVE

Robert Atkins as a Shakespearian Director

BY

ARTHUR COLBY SPRAGUE

(A lecture given at the Royal Shakespeare Theatre Summer School in August 1967. Extended and reprinted by kind permission from *Deutsche Shakespeare-Gesellschaft West Jahrbuch* 1973)

The death of Robert Atkins early in 1972 broke a strong link with the past. His own eighty-five years took us back to Henry Irving in London and Frank Benson at Stratford. Some of his stories concerned the theatre of a still earlier time. I remember his telling me of how he once asked Forbes-Robertson who was the greatest actor he had ever seen, and of how Forbes-Robertson startled him by saying, without hesitation, Samuel Phelps: and Phelps had once been a rival of Macready.

It was in a theatre still dominated by star actors that Atkins began his career, appearing several times with Martin Harvey, with Forbes-Robertson, and especially with Beerbohm Tree. With Tree he made his first professional appearance in 1906 and remained for some time under his management. There is more than a touch of irony in this. For Tree at innumerable points stood opposed to the man who was to influence Atkins most, William Poel. Atkins knew Poel well and though amused by his lapses into eccentricity always spoke of him with respect. Poel, he used to tell, would often stop at his flat to see him and he always gave him a glass of milk, Poel being the sort of man who would starve himself in order to produce one more play. Poel liked what Atkins did at the Old Vic and felt that standards there went down when he left. Indeed, much of what Atkins accomplished as a director came as the result of his adopting and making current ideas which he owed to Poel. But these ideas, it must be added, were carried out with a tact and good sense which their originator did not always possess. Atkins, moreover, for all his devotion to the Elizabethans and their stage, remained a hard-bitten professional. Accounts of his career are crowded with dates and engagements. There were, especially his five seasons

133

at the Old Vic (1920–1925); his two summers at Stratford-upon-Avon (1944 and 1945); and his long association with the outdoor theatre in Regent's Park, beginning in the 1930s and continuing, with only an occasional break, till 1961. One other, very brief engagement, during which he put on three of Shakespeare's plays for a few performances each, I shall take up in some detail near the end of this paper.

It was perhaps the most interesting of all.

It was once said of Atkins that although he 'did not make the Old Vic, he made it worth while'.[1] In particular his production of Ibsen's *Peer Gynt* attracted people who had not before visited this out-of-the-way, unfashionable playhouse; while for connoisseurs and collectors he offered a chance to see Shakespearian works which had not been given in London time out of mind, rarities like *Timon of Athens* and *Titus Andronicus*. In five seasons, he did in fact produce *Pericles*, and all of the First Folio plays except *Cymbeline* and *Measure for Measure*, though with the three parts of *Henry VI* compressed into two evenings. This last concession, one which later experience, notably at the Birmingham Repertory Theatre, shows to have been unnecessary, was exceptional. The relative fullness of the Old Vic texts is repeatedly mentioned at the time. Only the Alcibiades scenes in *Timon* shook the faith of one critic in what, with some exaggeration, he calls the 'settled plan of playing every play in its entirety.'[2] Another Atkins innovation, closely related, was the reduction in the number of intervals and the cutting down of such pauses as occurred between scenes. Thus in his first season *The Winter's Tale* had only two intervals, one of these short; *Twelfth Night* and *As You Like It* had two each; and *The Tempest* and *King John*, only one. In December 1922 an *Antony and Cleopatra* which included the rarely given scene on 'A plain in Syria', following the revelry on Pompey's galley, had again only a single interval.

What he accomplished is the more striking in view of the difficulties and restrictions which he had to overcome. The Old Vic, under Lilian Baylis, was only emerging now from what it had been, an enlightened social centre. Its proscenium stage did not accommodate itself to Elizabethan experiment. There was not much space, little rehearsal time, and desperately little money. My friend Leo Baker, who was with Atkins at this time, remembers being told to set the banquet in *Macbeth* and asking, naturally enough, how much he could spend. 'Anything you like, my boy', was the reply, 'up to a pound...'. As in Poel's productions, much of the action took place against plain curtains. One or two set scenes would be added. James Agate praises the scenery for *Richard III* as:

admirable throughout, by which I mean it was almost non-existent. A few bits of cardboard covered with brown paper made up a battlement:

some bigger bits, aided by good lighting, did for Richard's tent; the whole so imaginatively composed that it never got in the actor's way or stood between you and the play. I doubt whether the mounting cost a five pound note.[3]

A change by which the new director greatly profited was effected at the beginning of his second season. This was the sinking of the orchestra beneath a small apron-stage, enabling the actors to establish a greater measure of intimacy with the audience than had existed before. The King in *Love's Labour's Lost* addressed part of his opening monologue to them. Hay Petrie as Launce in *The Two Gentlemen of Verona* 'had the temerity to wink— actually to wink—at a gentleman in a side box.'[4] Such novelties are exciting to read of, whether we think of them as a return to Elizabethan practice or as anticipating certain experiments of our own time.

Some of the players who appeared under Atkins—George Hayes, Ernest Milton, Wilfrid Walter—I was to see and admire at a later time. Others like Ion Swinley and Florence Saunders I know only from descriptions of their acting. Atkins himself played a number of rôles, including Caliban, and Sir Toby, and one in which I should like to have seen him, Sir Giles Overreach in *A New Way to Pay Old Debts*. For the Company occasionally did something not by Shakespeare, though Shakespeare came first with them and with their audience, the still popular, largely local audience of The Old Vic.

Of the seasons which Atkins directed at Stratford-upon-Avon I have less to say. On 31 December 1943, before he had begun, *The Stratford-upon-Avon Herald* called attention to an important alteration at the Memorial Theatre:

The fore-stage, which is outside the proscenium arch and is normally lower than the stage proper has been raised to the level of the full stage... The actors can now approach to within a foot or so of the front row of the stalls without descending any steps.

The good effect of this change was evident at once in the opening scene of *The Merchant of Venice*. Mr. W. A. Darlington noted that although 'The young men on the stage were speaking at a normal pitch... their voices were coming clear and clean-cut to my ear.' It was only when the actors remained behind the proscenium arch that the acoustics remained obstinate.[5] Once more, as at the Old Vic, Atkins was seeking a greater degree of intimacy with the audience—'non-stop intimacy' was his phrase. And in *The Stratford-upon-Avon Herald* he expressed the hope that England would someday have 'A stage approximating to the stage in Shakespeare's time in which his plays can be fully listened to and not merely looked at.' 'I am an out-and-out Elizabethan', he added.[6]

In the course of his two seasons at Stratford Atkins produced sixteen plays, fourteen by Shakespeare, *She Stoops to Conquer* and *Volpone*. He was allowed to make a brief tour just before opening, and then to give only four—not eight plays—during the first fortnight. These would seem to have been regarded as major concessions in his favour. His productions did not attract much attention in their time. Likeliest to be referred to, nowadays, was an *Antony and Cleopatra*, given with a good deal of splendour. Claire Luce, an American actress for whom Atkins retained a high-regard, was Cleopatra. *Henry VIII* was also given (with George Skillan as Wolsey), but it was still wartime and understandably the familiar plays came first.

In 1945 Atkins resigned as head of the Company at Stratford and returned to his management of the theatre in Regent's Park. One of the curious gaps in stage history is that there is no book on the many productions of Shakespeare's plays out-of-doors. Going back in time to the later decades of the nineteenth century, these productions were both liberating and restrictive. As an alternative to representational scenery, to 'mossy banks' and stage trees, there was much to be said for a natural setting like that which Atkins found in Queen Mary's Gardens. But although this did admirably for some Shakespearian sequences it was less suitable for others. Even *A Midsummer Night's Dream* moves at length to an interior, that of the great house to which Theseus, the lovers, the would-be actors, and the fairies themselves come, near the end of the play.

Atkins made the most of a permanent background of trees and undergrowth. He added very little in the way of heavy properties. The ship at sea in *The Tempest* became in his 1949 production a tiny rocking-horse ship, beside which as it was drawn in, the lords and mariners walked gravely, while the surrounding waves were mimed by dancers. Nothing could have been more unlike the desperate and doomed attempts at realism in most earlier and some later productions.

At times he tried unfamiliar works: *Cymbeline* and *Pericles*; Milton's *Comus*; *The Faithful Shepherdess* by Fletcher; and what was called 'a miracle of smooth compression' a double bill made up of much-abridged versions of *The Comedy of Errors* and *The Two Gentlemen of Verona*. Increasingly, however, he turned to the safety of *Twelfth Night*, *A Midsummer Night's Dream*, and *The Tempest*, in each of which he found a major part for himself as an actor.

Of the three, Bottom the Weaver, Sir Toby Belch and Caliban, Atkins was best as Caliban. His Toby varied greatly from performance to performance. I remember seeing him in this rôle, soon after a revival of his *Twelfth Night* had opened, and being delighted. His appearance was most impressive. He might have stepped down from some seventeenth-century portrait of a burly nobleman. The character was consistent, and it was represented without exaggeration. Then, a few weeks later I saw it again, and found the actor introducing such tricks of his craft as the repeating of the last word or words spoken, with much comic grunting and clucking. It was wholly different. His Caliban was more original, more striking, and it varied, I believe, much less. Two moments stood out: The clumsy dance with which he accompanied his

'Ban, 'Ban, Ca-Caliban,
Has a new master—Get a new man;

and the speaking, still in character, but very musically, of the lines to Stephano beginning,

Be not afeard: the isle is full of noises,
Sounds, and sweet airs, that give delight and hurt not...

The Theatre in the Park was not one in which the ideals for which Atkins stood could hope to be realised. Wind and weather, the din of planes overhead, the mechanical amplification of the voices, all had to be overcome if Shakespeare's verse was to produce its effect; nor could his actors achieve much intimacy with their audience. He did what he could. After one very good performance, which I had just been praising, the comment of Mrs. Atkins was illuminating: 'I don't think there is a bad voice in the cast.' It was what William Poel might have remarked about some performance of which he approved.

I mentioned the fact that Atkins directed still another series of plays. This was in the winter of 1936–37, about midway between his last season at the Old Vic and his first at Stratford. It was a very brief season and the performances were on Sunday evenings. It opened significantly, with *Henry V*, November 29, to be followed by *Much Ado about Nothing* and *The Merry Wives of Windsor*. Among the players were: Violet and Irene Vanbrugh, as Mrs. Ford and Mrs. Page, with Roy Byford as their tormented Falstaff; Jack Hawkins as Benedick, and Margaretta Scott as Beatrice; and, in *Henry V*, Leslie French as the Chorus and Andrew Leigh as Fluellen. *Henry V* was of all the plays the right one with which to open, since Shakespeare through the Chorus is appealing to the imagination of the audience, who are to 'work' their thoughts and to share his vision. And the stage upon which it was now acted was a stage that attempted no impossible realisation in physical terms, a stage for poetry.

Atkins discovered it, not in any London theatre, or even hall, and not out-of-doors, but in the Prize Ring on Blackfriars Road, south of the river—not far from where the Swan Theatre once stood. Now a platform erected for prize fighting has to be fully visible to as many spectators as possible. An intense concentrated light, dazzling to those unaccustomed to it, shines down upon the contenders. At the Ring, Atkins found it unnecessary to employ more than half the overhead floods. His company were sparing of make-up and used only a little grease-paint. He reminds us (and the fact is not always remembered) that in Shakespeare's time 'the most important positions for the spectators were in the galleries, rather than on the floor of the theatre.' And at the boxing stadium it was those in the gallery who got 'the effect of the varied grouping of brightly coloured costumes, "framed" against the stage. The "picture stage" of the Elizabethans was this grouping of actors finely costumed.'[7]

The audience sat on three sides of a platform, almost bare of properties, at the back of which was a curtained structure, something like the Elizabethan tiring-house, with two doorways and a balcony. This balcony was used only once in *Henry V*, when the Governor of Harfleur appeared on it, as if upon the walls of the city. As adapted, the Ring yielded a stage 'thirty-four feet wide by thirty deep', an area somewhat smaller than that assumed for The Globe but by no means contemptible. The elevation of the platform by four feet combined happily with the proximity of the audience. It was a stage both intimate and removed.[8]

The reviews of these productions are of exceptional interest. Mr. Darlington in *The Daily Telegraph* stops short of wanting to have Shakespeare's dramas always performed in this way; but the novel staging at the boxing stadium gave them 'a liveliness and rightness which cannot be got elsewhere'. In particular the 'descriptive poetry, composed to take the place of scenery' assumed its true value in the 'brilliant performance' of Leslie French as Chorus. Mr. Ivor Brown in *The Observer* had faults to point out, but found that on such a stage as this the plays gained 'in speed, flexibility and intimacy'. He was persuaded, furthermore, 'that soliloquies are infinitely better spoken on a platform to a surrounding audience than from behind a proscenium arch'. The critic of *The Evening News* shared Darlington's view of the new importance of The Chorus: here was indeed the 'wooden O' of which he spoke, and the audience 'thrilled to the realisation'. Atkins himself must have perceived as much. For even before the prologue was completed he left the theatre, hurried across the street, and ordered a drink, adding (to the barman): 'Tim, I've got a hit.'

As was only natural, the second production at The Ring caused less excitement—though Herbert Farjeon spoke of its having knocked 'every other production of *Much Ado* into a cocked hat.'[9] That of *The Merry Wives of Windsor*, however, if only because of the obvious strength of its cast, led to some consideration of the relationships which the new staging bore to acting. Ivor Brown was now more cordial than he had been before.

He found, it is true, rather loss than gain in the absence of scenery; but the bringing of the players into the midst of the audience was warmly welcomed: 'We are friendly participants, not detached spectators.' And what an advantage to have a great actress like Irene Vanbrugh 'right before us instead of set back in the cold framework of the proscenium arch'. There had previously been complaints on inaudibility—acoustics do not come first, we may suppose, with the designers of prize rings—but in this production the voices of Falstaff and the Wives came through beautifully. The good actors had stood the test.[10]

The most thoughtful criticism of The Blackfriars Road Venture came from a somewhat unexpected source. On 9 December 1936 Desmond Macarthy in *The New Statesman and Nation* had praised an Old Vic production of *The Witch of Edmonton* as having 'caught the spirit of that drama so completely and projected it so vividly (thanks to a most judicious use of modern pictorial devices) that, speaking for myself, the performance has unskinned my eyes'. And he went on to assert that no production of a play by Shakespeare or one of his fellows which did not catch its atmosphere was of any value; nor can atmosphere be 'achieved by reproducing *as exactly as possible* the conditions of the Elizabethan and Jacobean stage'. Now Geoffrey Tillotson (later to become Professor of English Literature in the University of London) took issue with this as implying the rejection in favour of 'the picture stage' of what Atkins was accomplishing 'with a scratch team of Sunday-evening actors' and, by way of stage, 'the actual ring of the boxing stadium with a balcony ... at one end.'[11]

Tillotson would have, not one method of presenting the plays of Shakespeare and his fellows, but two, both of them indispensable, 'the Elizabethan way and the modern'. Those who in any age are seeking 'new principles, methods and effects' should be free to apply them to 'Elizabethan poetic drama'; and indeed at the hands of such producers 'Shakespeare's plays have always been found legitimately turning into new plays, 'to the delight of' audiences Augustan, Victorian or modern—and he cites some of Tyrone Guthrie's recent work.

But because this kind of new production has always drawn its producers and audiences, it need not exclude the Elizabethan kind. And this not simply because the Elizabethan kind is the only one that can recreate effects in the plays which otherwise remain puzzling, because only this method can show us why Shakespeare carpentered his plays just as he did. But also because there can be no doubt that both Shakespeare (the poet-dramatist) and his actors get their due from Mr. Atkins in a way that they do not from 'modern' producers. The words of the plays mean

far more to an audience for whom they and the physical presence of the
actors are almost the only channel for the grand total of the play. In the
Victorian productions the romatically elaborated realism of the setting
sirened attention away from the words, and though modern sirens are
more fashionable, they are sirens still. At the Ring there is no scenery,
and the audience, which almost surrounds the actors, watches the
actors and receives their words with an unencumbered directness of
attention which gives its proper meaning to the term 'poetic drama'.
It is because of this literary and human focus, that in Mr. Atkins's
productions, scenery is not missed.

If I have placed a very heavy emphasis on these three productions it is
because of my feeling of their importance and comparative neglect. For
once Atkins had a free hand; for once was able to give Shakespeare's
plays nearly as he wanted to give them. There was no trace of antiquarian-
ism about this venture (Atkins liked, I am sure, the boxing ring atmosphere).
In 1953, nevertheless, Richard Southern could write of 'these now famous
presentations' that in them Atkins 'tried in practice the real, open stage of
the Elizabethans as scarcely any modern besides him has been able to do.'[12]
Certain ideas and ideals keep appearing in the work of Robert Atkins.
Many of them, I suggested, go back to Poel. Some of them are still very
much alive today. Belief in the value of a complete, or relatively complete
text is among these. The impoverishment of Shakespeare in the usual acting
editions of his plays at the close of the nineteenth century was pointed out
repeatedly by Poel. Granville-Barker's very full texts of *The Winter's Tale*,
Twelfth Night, and *A Midsummer Night's Dream*, at the Savoy Theatre, just
before the First World War, helped to set a standard; and at Stratford, there
was W. Bridges-Adams, to maintain it—not for nothing was he sometimes
called 'Un-abridges Adams'. When, accordingly, Atkins gave many of
Shakespeare's plays uncut he had precedent for what he did. That popular
audiences at the Old Vic were ready to accept them fifty years ago is not the
less remarkable.
Chiefly to blame for the deplorable state of the text was the use of heavy
sets and the time taken to change them. Audiences were accustomed
to frequent waits and long ones, accepting them as a matter of course. A
reader here and there might be disturbed by what he found missing, but any
momentary objection of his would be silenced when he recalled the magnifi-
cence of this or that production under one of the great actor-managers.
Then, too, were not these scenes, historically and topographically exact as
they often purported to be, educational as well as spectacular, and a mark
of progress? That the whole shape of the play had been altered, he could

scarcely be expected to perceive, Shakespeare's extraordinary skill as a playwright was only beginning to be asserted. It still awaited practical demonstration. And a fuller text required lighter scenery, or even a bare stage. As we saw, Atkins compromised at the Old Vic, employing in the same production Poel's plain curtains and scenic sets. At last, at the Prize Ring, he freed himself wholly from the nineteenth century.

The intimacy between stage and audience which existed in Shakespeare's theatre was something which he sought to regain throughout his career. In this matter he owed little to anyone else. Poel sometimes had recourse to entrances through the audience. These, we now know, can be extraordinarily impressive (I am remembering *Hadrian VII* at the Mermaid Theatre and many instances at Stratford, Ontario). When, however, Poel had his Chorus in *Samson Agonistes* come down through the audience it was to send Max Beerbohm, as the latter tells us, into 'paroxysms of internal laughter'. Seeking a closer contact between stage and stalls, Atkins, in his turn, made structural changes, first, as we saw, at the Old Vic, later at Stratford-upon-Avon. It was only, once more, when he hit upon the idea of creating a new stage out of the boxing ring, that he succeeded. In an article published in 1955 he pointed out that 'most modern producers' had come to recognize the importance of something like a complete text, 'and continuity of action'; and for this advance he felt that he might 'claim a little credit'. He wrote also of a theatre in which Shakespeare's plays might be performed to the best advantage; not 'an archaeological reconstruction' of the Elizabethan playhouse but a building which retained its essentials, 'the forward platform ... Intimacy! Intimacy! Intimacy!'[13]

I have tried not to exaggerate the claims to be made on behalf of Robert Atkins as a Shakespearian director. How seriously you take these claims will depend, I suggest, on how well you are acquainted with his career, especially with the early years at the Old Vic and the brief experiment on the Blackfriars Road; also, it may be on your attitude toward the open stage whether, that is to say, you cling to the staging of yesterday and the day before, to the proscenium arch and substantial scenery, or desire, as Atkins desired, a renewed intimacy between audience and actors, something like that of the Elizabethans. Through many years Atkins belonged among the innovators, was a follower of the new ways with Shakespeare. There is irony then, a sad irony, in the fact that toward the end of his life he came to be thought of, rather widely, as that quaint character, the typical 'old actor', about whom one told funny stories.

Yet from another point of view it is not easy to think of Robert Atkins as a rebel. He seems strangely cast in that rôle. Indeed, except in matters of staging, one did not look for anything radically new in a production of his.

Not that he was without ideas. For him, as for many of his contemporaries, the author's intention, Shakespeare's intention, was all-important, and this an actor might discern where scholars had failed (he did not much like scholars). I attended only one rehearsal conducted by him. It was of a late *Hamlet* which he was preparing to give in Lebanon. When we reached the King's opening speech,

> *Though yet of Hamlet our dear brother's death*
> *The memory be green . . .*

he interrupted, abruptly—'No, no, no!'—and hurried forward from where he had been standing. 'This', he explained to the actor, 'is your first speech since you've been made king, and you don't know how they will take it. Watch their eyes. Feel your way. If any of them look suspicious, off with their heads! Liquidate them! Siberia!' I should like to believe that such criticism as this was typical of Atkins as a director. For it was fresh and imaginative.

On one matter he was endlessly insistent, the accurate delivery of the verse. This, to a remarkable degree, he succeeded in teaching the actors whom he rehearsed. Norman Marshall writes that he had never known an actor who had once 'worked with Atkins who did not understand and respect the rhythm of Shakespeare's verse'.[14] It is a remarkable tribute. In the spring of 1944 Atkins spoke to the members of the Stratford-upon-Avon Shakespeare Club on himself and his beliefs. He was, he reminded his hearers, 'The only man living in London who had produced every play attributed to William Shakespeare'. And what had he learned from his experience? This, 'that the only thing that mattered was the spoken word'.[15]

Endnotes

[1] Herbert Farjeon, *The Shakespearian Scene* (1949), p. 133.
[2] *The Weekly Westminster Gazette*, 13.5.1922.
[3] *The Contemporary Theatre* (1924), pp. 80, 81.
[4] Farjeon, *op. cit.*, p. 183.
[5] *The Daily Telegraph*, 10.4.1944.
[6] *The Stratford-upon-Avon Herald*, 21.1.1944.
[7] Much of this description is based on a valuable article by Atkins. 'Shakespeare on his Stage', in *The Amateur Theatre and Playwright's Journal*, ed. John Bourne, 19.4.1937.
[8] Information supplied by Mr. Jack Reading of the Society for Theatre Research, who saw the production.
[9] Farjeon, *op. cit*, p. 35.
[10] *The Manchester Guardian*, 15.3.1937.
[11] *Essays in Criticism and Research*, Cambridge, 1942, pp. 48–52.
[12] *The Open Stage* (1953), p. 38.
[13] 'Memories and Reflections', *Plays and Players*, April 1955.
[14] *The Producer and the Play*, revised edition, 1962, p. 260.
[15] *The Stratford-upon-Avon Herald*, 5.5.1944.

From Who's Who in the Theatre

14th EDITION, 1967

ATKINS, Robert, C.B.E., actor and stage director; *b.* Dulwich, 10 August 1886; *s.* of Robert Atkins and his wife Annie (Evans); *e.* privately; *m.* (1) Mary Sumner (mar. dis.); (2) Ethel Davey (dec.); was a pupil at the Academy of Dramatic Art, 1905–6, and walked on at His Majesty's Theatre, January 1906, in the production of *Nero*; at a public performance of the pupils of the Academy at His Majesty's Theatre, April 1906, made quite a hit as Shylock in the trial scene from *The Merchant of Venice*, and as M. Pierrot in *L'Enfant Prodigue*; on the strength of this performance was engaged by the late Sir Herbert Tree for His Majesty's, and remained under his management for three years; he made his first appearance in a speaking part there, 24 April 1906, as Henry Percy in *King Henry IV* (Part I), and subsequently he played Marcellus in *Hamlet*, Bowkins in *Colonel Newcome*, Bishop of Carlisle in *Richard II*, Ventidius in *Antony and Cleopatra*, the Old Shepherd in *The Winter's Tale*, the Sea Captain in *Twelfth Night*, Metellus Cimber in *Julius Caesar*, the Dean of Cloisterham in *The Mystery of Edwin Drood*, M. Dubois in *The Beloved Vagabond*, Duke of Venice in *The Merchant of Venice*, Master Page in *The Merry Wives of Windsor*, First Actor in *Hamlet*, the Burgomaster in *Faust*; played for one season at the Repertory Theatre, Glasgow; subsequently toured with Martin Harvey, and appeared with him at the Lyceum Theatre, May 1911, as the Public Prosecutor in *The Only Way*; he then joined Forbes-Robertson, and after touring appeared with him at Drury Lane Theatre, March–May 1913, as Marcellus and the First Player in *Hamlet*, Phil Raynor in *The Light that Failed*, Centurion in *Caesar and Cleopatra*, Balthazar in *The Merchant of Venice*, and Ludovico in *Othello*; he then accompanied Forbes-Robertson to the United States; also toured for some time with Sir Frank Benson's Shakespearian companies; in October 1915, he joined the company of the Old Vic, and appeared as Jaques in *As You Like It*, Prince of Verona in *Romeo and Juliet*, Antonio in *The Merchant of Venice*, Iago in *Othello*, Richard in *Richard III*, Macbeth, Sir Toby Belch in *Twelfth Night*, Prospero in *The Tempest*, Cassius in *Julius Caesar*, etc.; he also appeared with the company at the Memorial Theatre, Stratford-on-Avon; after being demobilized from the Army, 1919, he toured with Ben Greet's company; he returned to the Old Vic in September 1920, as director, and also appeared there as King Lear, Caliban in *The Tempest*, Richard III, Sir Toby Belch in *Twelfth Night*, etc.; went with the company to the Parc Theatre, Brussels, June 1921, at the invitation of the Belgian Government; at the Old Vic November 1922, played Sir Giles Overreach in a revival of *A New Way to Pay Old Debts*; at the same theatre, he also revived Shakespeare's *King Henry VI* (Parts I, II, and III), *Titus Andronicus*, and *Troilus and Cressida*, plays but rarely revived during the past century, besides several original plays; in addition he staged *Peer Gynt*, for the first time in England; at the New Oxford Theatre, June 1924, with the Old Vic company, produced *The Taming of the Shrew*, *Hamlet*, *As You Like It*, and *Twelfth Night*; at the Old Vic, June 1925, revived Pinero's *Trelawny of the "Wells"*, in which he played James Telfer, and then concluded his long association with that theatre; entered on the management of the New Theatre, 7 July 1925, when he directed Zangwill's *We Moderns*; during 1926 staged several plays at Everyman and 'Q' Theatres; appeared at the Little Theatre, October 1926, in *Potinière Revue*, and at the Globe, November 1926, as James Telfer in *Trelawny of the "Wells"*; in 1927 formed the Forum Theatre Guild, and directed at the Royalty, March 1927, *Cocks and Hens*, and April 1927, *The Dybbuk*; at the St. James's May 1927, directed *Twelfth Night* for the Forbes-Robertson 'Clan' *matinée*, and played Sir Toby Belch; in October 1927, took his own company to Egypt, playing Shakespearean Repertory, and paid a second visit October–December 1928; at the Strand Theatre (for the Stage Society), April 1929, directed and played the title-*rôle* in *Rasputin*; at the Haymarket and Apollo, July 1929, played Mr. Ford in *The Merry Wives of Windsor* (in modern dress); directed *Barren Gain*, 1929; *Ruth*, *Search*, and *The Passing of the Essenes*, 1930; *If*, *The Mantle*, and *Measure for Measure*, 1931; at the New Theatre, April 1932, played Napoleon in Drinkwater's adaptation of Mussolini's play of that name, which he also directed; New, May 1932, played Sir Toby Belch in *Twelfth Night*, which he directed; Ambassadors', November 1932, Professor Venables in *Philomel*, which he directed; at the Arts, November 1932, directed *All's Well that Ends Well*; Westminster, March 1933, *Caesar's Friend*; Arts, March 1933, *Bellairs*; Open Air Theatre, June–September 1933, played Sir Toby Belch in *Twelfth Night*; Bottom in *A Midsummer Night's Dream* and Caliban in *The Tempest*; Wyndham's, December 1933, Fatty Bill in *What Happened to George*; Open Air

Theatre, June 1934, again played Bottom; July 1934, Ferrovius in *Androcles and the Lion*; Open Air, June–September 1935, Sir Toby Belch, Bottom, etc.; Open Air, June 1938, again played Caliban; August 1938, again played Sir Toby Belch and September 1938, Bottom; Winter Garden, May 1939, appeared as Macbeth; *Dance Macabre*, Arts, 1934; *Love is the Best Doctor*, Winter Garden, 1934; *Henry IV* (part I), His Majesty's, 1935; *Everyman*, Ambassadors', 1935; *Her Last Adventure*, Ambassadors', 1936; *Henry V*, *Much Ado About Nothing*, and *The Merry Wives of Windsor*, Ring, Blackfriars, 1936–7; directed *The History of the Drama from Sophocles to Shaw*, at the Coronation Costume Ball, Royal Albert Hall, May 1937; directed all the plays at the Open Air Theatre, 1933–43; was appointed manager of the Open Air Theatre, 1939, as well as Director; directed *Henry V*, at Stratford-on-Avon, April 1934, and *Othello*, April 1939; Palace, July 1940, staged the revival of *Chu-Chin-Chow*; Vaudeville, October 1940, directed *All's Well That Ends Well*, playing Lafeu, and *King Henry IV* (Part I), playing Falstaff; Open Air, August 1941, played Grumio in *The Taming of the Shrew*, Michael Williams in *King Henry V*, and Sir Toby in *Twelfth Night*; at the Westminster, September–December 1942, played Shylock, Falstaff, and Bottom; Open Air, August 1943, Caliban in *The Tempest*; Director of Productions of the Memorial Theatre, Stratford-on-Avon, 1944–5; directed sixteen plays there, and in June 1944, appeared as Volpone in Ben Jonson's play; resigned August 1945; directed *Golden Eagle* at the Westminster, 1946; also directed *Drake's Drum*, Embassy, 1946; has continued his annual seasons at the Open Air Theatre since that date; in addition to plays previously revived there, directed *Lady Precious Stream*, 1947; *As You Like It*, in which he played Touchstone, and *King John*, 1948; at the Fortune, December 1948, played Long John Silver in *Treasure Island*; at the Open Air Theatre directed *Much Ado About Nothing*, *The Comedy of Errors*, *The Two Gentlemen of Verona*, and *Faust*, 1949; *The Winter's Tale*, playing Autolycus, and *The Merchant of Venice*, playing Shylock, 1950; in May 1951, directed *A Midsummer Night's Dream*, playing Bottom; at the New, April 1952, played Thomas Parry in *The Young Elizabeth*; at the Open Air Theatre, 1952, directed *As You Like It*, *Cymbeline*, and *Comus*; in 1953, directed *Twelfth Night*, playing Sir Toby Belch; in 1955, directed *A Midsummer Night's Dream*, playing Bottom, *The Romanticks*, playing Bergamin, and appeared as Caliban in *The Tempest*; in 1956, directed *As You Like It*, *The Romanticks*, playing Bergamin, *Twelfth Night*, playing Sir Toby Belch; at the Baalbek Festival, Lebanon, August 1956, he directed his own company in *Hamlet*, and

Twelfth Night playing Sir Toby Belch; at the Open Air Theatre, Regent's Park, 1958, he directed *Much Ado About Nothing*, playing Dogberry, and appeared as Baptista in *The Taming of the Shrew*; in 1959, directed *Twelfth Night*, playing Sir Toby Belch, *A Midsummer Night's Dream*, playing Bottom; in 1960, directed *The Tempest*, playing Caliban, and *Tobias and the Angel*; Pembroke, Croydon, October 1960, directed and played Polonius in *Hamlet*; Edinburgh Festival, Lyceum, August 1961, played the Old Man and Gluttony in *Dr. Faustus*, and Austria in *King John*, with the Old Vic Company; Theatre Royal, Stratford, E., December 1962, directed *The Pied Piper*; Hippodrome, Brighton, June 1963, co-directed *Bogey 7*; in March 1933, received the honour of Knighthood (Cavaliere) of the Order of the Crown of Italy, in connection with his production of Signor Mussolini's play *Napoleon*; received the C.B.E. in the Birthday Honours, 1949; received the Lebanese Order of the Cedar, 1956; first appeared in films, 1935, in *Peg of Old Drury*; was appointed Director of the British Empire Shakespeare Society, 1927. *Recreation:* Golf.

Index

Index

Index

154